YOUNG ACTIVISTS
and the **Public Library**

YOUNG ACTIVISTS

and the **Public Library**

FACILITATING DEMOCRACY

VIRGINIA A. WALTER

ALA Editions

CHICAGO 2020

VIRGINIA A. WALTER worked for more than twenty years in public libraries before starting her second career as a library educator at UCLA. She is now an emerita professor who teaches one class a year on some topic related to children's or young adult librarianship. She has written or coauthored ten professional books. Her recent titles include *5 Steps of Outcome-Based Planning and Evaluation* with Melissa Gross and Cindy Mediavilla (2016) and *Transforming Summer Programs at Your Library* with Natalie Cole (2018).

Extensive effort has gone into ensuring the reliability of the information in this book; however, the publisher makes no warranty, express or implied, with respect to the material contained herein.

ISBN: 978-0-8389-4738-8 (paper)

Library of Congress Control Number: 2020000808

Cover design by Alejandra Diaz. Cover image © Good Studio, Adobe Stock.

⊚ This paper meets the requirements of ANSI/NISO Z39.48-1992 (Permanence of Paper).

Printed in the United States of America

24 23 22 21 20   5 4 3 2 1

Contents

Introduction | *vii*

CHAPTER 1

Young People, Civic Literacy, and Libraries

1

CHAPTER 2

Information for Young Activists

19

CHAPTER 3

Putting Civic Literacy to Work

Engaging Children and Teens as Active Participants in Their Communities

35

CHAPTER 4

Resources for Civic Literacy

45

Conclusion | *95*

References | *97*

Index | *103*

Introduction

Born in 1943, I am a part of what is often called the Silent Generation. It is true that I saw no need or opportunity to raise my voice until my late teens. As a little girl, I heard radio broadcasts of the McCarthy hearings and felt an unease I couldn't articulate. I felt a frisson of fear when I saw a jet plane fly over our home in Saint Paul; I participated in frequent "duck and cover drills" intended to prepare us for a nuclear attack. I read about political events in *My Weekly Reader*. However, it never occurred to me that I could do anything about these events or even form an opinion about them. My teen years brought an awareness of the civil rights movement but no understanding that the struggle of black Americans for their rights was my struggle too. I wish I had seen myself in those days as a potential ally of the oppressed and an activist working for a better world.

This book was born out of my respect and admiration for the young survivors of the Parkland High School shooting. They did not mourn their fallen classmates in passive silence. Instead they raised their voices and organized young people across the country to march for their lives. Like Greta Thunberg more recently, they accused adults in power of letting their generation down.

The time is right for young people—children as well as teens—to take a stand and try to fix what is broken in their world: global climate change, racism, homophobia, a culture of violence, inequality and injustice of all kinds. The time is right for adults to work with them. Public libraries are uniquely situated to help young people restore the democratic values and ideals to which we all aspire. This book offers both a rationale for a more activist role for public libraries and some strategies for achieving it by supporting the civic engagement of our young patrons.

Chapter 1 is a sweeping look at the phenomenon of youth activism in this country and around the world, at the emerging concept of civic literacy, and at the role public libraries can play in nurturing the activism of our young patrons. You will find many references to scholars and professionals who have informed my thinking. I hope you will find some of these so interesting and stimulating that you follow up and read some of the works cited.

Chapter 2 is more practical—it provides examples and strategies to help you help the children and teens you serve become more informed about their rights and obligations as citizens. Because public librarians do not have the daily contact or the mandate to educate that teachers do, we have to look for other ways to make meaningful and important ideas available to young people. Sometimes a kid will ask a reference question that is directly relevant to civic engagement and strong democracy. More often, though, we have to intuit the unasked question. The whole concept of civic engagement carries more than a hint of liberal political ideology, and we need to be careful not to overstep our bounds as providers of neutral information. Within the parameters of our professional ethics, however, there are ways we can use our role as information provider to arm young people with the resources they need to think for themselves and make good decisions about the issues that affect them.

Chapter 3 moves beyond strategies for providing information to strategies for creating opportunities for children and teens to practice the skills of democracy and to participate actively in civic life. Here is where public libraries can really live up to their potential as a third space, mediating between the personal life of home and the public life of our community, state, and nation. There are examples in this chapter that are drawn from real-life programs and initiatives. You can learn from things that are being tried in other public libraries. However, I have also suggested some initiatives for encouraging participation that may not have been tried. I hope some librarians out there find these inspiring and worthwhile enough to test them. If so, please take the time to write about them for publications like *American Libraries*, *Public Libraries*, *Children and Libraries*, or *Young Adult Library Services*. We can create a kind of community of practice by sharing our innovative ideas for services and programs with other professionals in the public library world.

Chapter 4 is a lengthy list of print resources to get you started thinking about specific titles you can share with kids. This resource list is arranged according to subject—topics like children and activism, as well as issues that young people are passionate about, such as gun control and the environment. This is not an exhaustive list, but it should be a springboard that gets you thinking about other resources you might draw on. I have not included websites or other digital resources because the most useful ones are often very fluid and time sensitive. You have the skills to locate these yourself if you and your young patrons need them.

Finally, the conclusion is my last chance to remind you how important you are to the young people you serve, and to encourage you to take a more activist role yourself in fostering the democratic values and ideals we all aspire to.

Young People, Civic Literacy, and Libraries

Young Activists Today

Something is happening all around the world: children and teens are stand-ing up and speaking out about their determination to make changes in the world they have inherited from us adults.

In September of 2019, Hong Kong police arrested a fifteen-year-old boy who was wearing a black T-shirt and surgical mask, like so many of the young people who have been protesting there against efforts by the Chinese government to limit political freedoms. As it happens, he was not a protester; he was just dressed like one. Apparently that is enough to warrant arrest now in Hong Kong. Denise Hoe, a singer and activist, said, "Young people merely dressed in black can be searched and even arrested without justification. In other words, merely being young is a crime in the police state of Hong Kong." Of the 1,596 people arrested since the beginning of the protests in June 2018, 404 were students (Su and Kilpatrick 2019).

Earlier that month, millions of people from all around the world participated in a global climate strike. This was a protest inspired and organized primarily by young people. It was initiated by a sixteen-year-old Swedish girl named Greta Thunberg. The *New York Times* published a full page with photos and profiles of young people who participated in Uganda, Mumbai, Cape Town, London, and La Paz, as well as New York. Leah Namugerwa, a fifteen-year-old from Kampala, Uganda, said "I noticed adults were not willing to offer leadership, and I chose to volunteer myself." Two young people from Cape Town talked about how the drought there has precipitated a crisis with contaminated water. Nineteen-year-old Adriana Salazar from La Paz, Bolivia, worries about the drought in that country that has produced devastating forest fires and mass immigration from rural areas to the cities. "I don't know what world my kids will live in. The kids, the indigenous communities, pregnant women, they'll see the effects while the higher classes will avoid the worst of it," she said (Sengupta 2019).

The organizers of the global climate strikes presented a complaint to the United Nations Committee on the Rights of the Child for violating the rights of children who are "victims of the pollution that's been carelessly dumped into our land, air and sea for generations." That quote is from Alexandria Villasenor, a teenager who was visiting family in Northern California when fires killed eighty-six people and destroyed fifteen thousand homes. Alexandria's asthma was triggered by the fire and resulted in a trip to the emergency room. She began to research wildfires and their connection to asthma. Back in New York, she began sitting outside the United Nations building every Friday, protesting in solidarity with Greta Thunberg and other young activists (Shalby 2019).

The effectiveness of this youthful protest resulted in some scathing backlash from the right-wing media. Among the critics was Laura Ingraham, a Fox News host, who said that Ms. Thunberg "deserved a spanking or an intervention" (Warzel 2019). Even President Donald Trump weighed in after Thunberg's UN speech, in which she seemed to hold back tears as she attacked world leaders for ignoring the threat of climate change. In a sarcastic tweet, Trump said, "She seems like a very happy young girl looking forward to a bright and wonderful future. So nice to see!" (Stracqualursi 2019). Thunberg, unflappable as always, said at a rally in Montreal, "That we should take as a compliment, that we are having so much impact that people want to silence us" (*LA Times*, 2019).

The global climate strikes were just the latest in a series of youth-propelled movements to combat the environmental threats posed by climate change. Young plaintiffs are suing the United States government for violating their constitutional rights. *Juliana v. United States* argues that the federal government "has created a national energy system that causes climate change, is depriving them of their constitutional rights to life, liberty, and property and [failing] to protect essential public trust resources" (Walrath 2018). In June 2019, the Ninth Circuit Court of Appeals heard the case and the counterarguments presented by the government. In January 2020, the court dismissed the case, but the plaintiffs plan to appeal the court's decision.

Portland, Oregon, the birthplace of *Juliana v. United States*, is also the site of one of the first American school districts to integrate climate change and justice into the curriculum of all its schools. This was the result of a three-year effort by students who argued for a focus not just on global warming but on people in frontline communities. Sriya Chinnam, a Portland high school student, explained, "With natural disasters, communities of color will be hit the hardest. Because they'll be in places where they don't have the type of infrastructure to help them rebuild their homes and help them adapt" (Seely 2019).

A less well-publicized national movement is Zero Hour, organized by teenagers who were inspired by other youth-led movements such as the March for Our Lives. With the initial funding of a $16,000 grant from the Common Sense Fund, the students have gone on to raise an additional $70,000 for their campaign to convince businesses to integrate ethical and sustainable environmental policies into their operating plans (Yoon-Hendricks 2018).

If climate change is the latest issue to motivate young people to organize and protest in the United States, it is not the first cause to galvanize them. The killing of seventeen students at Marjory Stoneman Douglas High School in Parkland, Florida, resulted in some new young activist leaders—Emma González, David Hogg, and others—and the remarkable March for Our Lives (Jarvie 2018). A *New York Times* reporter, Maggie Astor (2018), spent three days with the students on the March for Our Lives that the Parkland students organized to call attention to the relationship between gun control and school safety. Her report starts at the International Civil Rights Center & Museum in Greensboro, North Carolina. There, the March for Our Lives activists saw an installation of the Woolworth's lunch counter where students participated in a sit-in protest nearly sixty years before. For these teens, that lunch counter was a significant reminder of the difference people can make when confronted with injustice or wrongs in a society. The tour guide, Dillon Tyler, told the marchers that his school had been shot up twelve years before. One by one, the visiting students came forward and hugged him as he cried at the memory. Astor writes that these high school students shared the knowledge that any of them could be next; a group of fifteen-year-olds talked about which classrooms in their schools had good escape routes secured.

The school shooting whose impact on young people was articulated so powerfully by the surviving Parkland students generated protests around the issue of gun control among even elementary school students, many of whom participated in the National School Walkout in March 2018 (Saul and Hartocollis

2018). Others, like the young people in Newtown, Connecticut, have a personal experience with a gunman at their school. In 2012—five years before the Parkland shooting—Sandy Hook Elementary School was the place where twenty first graders and six adults were shot to death (Ray 2019). The oldest survivors of that massacre are now in high school and are beginning to join with others to speak out. They have organized voter registration drives and lobbied elective officials to ban semiautomatic weapons and close loopholes in laws for background checks (Hussey 2018).

Of course, Parkland was not the first site of a mass shooting in a public high school. The shooting at Columbine High School in Colorado in 1999 called national attention to the issue but did not result in any gun control legislation. Active shooter drills have taken the place of legislation to get weapons of mass destruction out of the hands of potential killers. The National Association of School Psychologists and the National Association of School Resource Officers have issued a manual of best practices for schools conducting active shooter and other armed assailant drills. The manual recommends that schools implement lockdowns as the foundation to active assailant training as the basis for an options-based approach. They note that the "Run, Hide, Fight" model is probably the most widely used option. They also urge schools to tailor their drills to individual developmental levels and to consider prior traumatic experiences when designing drills (NASP and NASRO 2014). Recently, however, there has been some pushback from parents and child psychologists to the widespread, often poorly conceived active shooter drills happening in schools. These less-effective drills may terrify already anxious children. Experts in both child psychology and security are now advising schools to take a more holistic approach to safeguarding children from gun violence. Such an approach would also attempt to make the school environment itself safer and to encourage more community-based mental health initiatives that would conduct threat assessments and treatment in advance before an individual tried to gain access to the school with a gun (Williamson 2019).

Public libraries have also been conducting active shooter training for staff since at least 2015. Public libraries, after all, are open to everybody, with most buildings lacking any metal detectors or requirements for handbag inspection. As with training for school staff, the focus appears to be on the "Run, Hide, Fight" model. The training seems to be limited to staff; I have found no documentation of drills conducted with patrons in the library (Moeller-Peiffer 2015). It is not clear that the special needs of children and teens are considered in any of these trainings. This might be an area for children's and teen librarians to get involved.

The issue of gun violence has not lost its urgency as time has passed. In May 2019, the Youth Council to End Gun Violence, an initiative of Los Angeles mayor Eric Garcetti, launched Louder Than Guns, a website and ad campaign. The campaign hopes to generate a wider, ongoing discussion of gun violence beyond the usual knee-jerk reaction to the latest mass shooting (Kohli 2019). As seventeen-year-old Tyler Okeke pointed out, many young people in Los Angeles experience violence on a nearly daily basis. Kevin, a sixteen-year-old who goes to a school surrounded by three gang territories, said that he and his friends even fear making the wrong hand movements in case someone thinks they are flashing gang signs. "It's something that I don't want to live in when I grow up and it's something that I don't want my little sisters and my little brothers to experience," he said (Lopez 2019).

Students at Palisades Charter High School in Los Angeles were part of a national team of teen journalists who created obituaries of young victims who were killed by guns in the 365 days after the Parkland shooting. The Palisades students live in an affluent, relatively safe community, but their research connected them with young people in places where the victims are often low-income persons of color. One of the young reporters noted that learning the details of the shootings made her angry and determined to get even more involved (Lopez 2019). The Palisades students were part of the "Since Parkland" project for which the Trace (a nonprofit news organization dedicated to reporting on gun violence) worked with high school journalism teachers to provide the young reporters with training and editing. The goal was to put a human face on the statistics and to generate awareness of the everyday impact guns have on children and teens (Ofori-Atta et al., n.d.).

African American and Latinx teens—especially those living in lower-income, urban areas—share many of the concerns of young people everywhere in the United States and other developed countries. However, they also have some unique situations to deal with. Andreana Clay (2012) has conducted an interesting in-depth study of students of color in Oakland, California. She spent time as a participant observer with students at two high schools where students of color are in the majority. She worked particularly with teens involved in two organizations: Teen Justice and Multicultural Alliance. She found that the teens were both inspired and intimidated by the legacy of past activists of color like Angela Davis, Malcolm X, and Che Guevara. There are still adults living in their community who were active in the Black Panthers. The teens have been exposed to a lot of consumer goods as well as mass media that focuses on charismatic, visionary activists of the past—T-shirts and posters with images of Huey Newton and Angela Davis, for example. Clay calls this an "idealized cultural image" of social and political activism (10). Many teens talked about the Black Panthers as role models whose commitment and accomplishments they aspired to emulate. Others, however, felt that those expectations were too high. When Clay asked one Latina teen if she thought of herself as an activist, she demurred, "I see more of an activist as someone who is out there protesting and I don't know, I don't feel that I do enough to become an activist. . . . I feel like an activist is someone who does a lot and spends all of his or her time trying to change stuff" (161).

Whether these Oakland teens saw themselves as activists or as less-involved participants in social change, they seemed united in their identity as members of the hip-hop generation. They found that their shared knowledge and love of this form of music connected them to one another and to other students that they wanted to attract to join them. The students involved in Teen Justice were working toward the establishment of a youth center at their high school. The teens affiliated with Multicultural Alliance were conducting anti-oppression workshops for other young people. Both organizations offered a lot of leadership development training in addition to providing opportunities for youth participation.

Latinx teens also have a legacy of activism. In 1968, hundreds of students at Garfield High School in East Los Angeles walked out of class. They were soon followed by similar "blowouts," as the students called them, at nearby Roosevelt and Lincoln High Schools. More than twenty-two thousand teens would participate in these protests over the coming weeks, supported by the recently formed Brown Berets. The students presented a list of demands to the Los Angeles school board: smaller classes; new libraries; more bilingual counselors, teachers, and principals; more teaching about Mexican American culture, art, and history. It would take years before significant change was reached, but many of the teens who participated in the blowouts continued their active civic engagement into their adult years. Pete Martinez, a teacher at Lincoln High School at the time, said, "In 1968, the kids kicked the doors open" (Sahagun 2018).

More recently, immigration rights have been a focus for many teens. Many who were brought to this country illegally as children have been shielded from some of the consequences of their lack of documentation by DACA—Deferred Action for Child Arrivals, a policy put in place during the Obama administration that affects nearly a million people currently living in the United States. For those eligible, it grants a two-year renewable exemption from deportation and the ability to get a work permit. Some states grant additional benefits to DACA recipients. California, for example, allows DACA individuals who pay taxes to get a driver's license and apply for Medi-Cal. The Trump administration has challenged the legality of the DACA policy, and at the time of writing, the Supreme Court is deciding the case (Blitzer 2019). Just minutes after the initial hearing for the case ended, demonstrations began around the country. In Los Angeles, hundreds of teens walked out of class as they urged the court to continue the policy (Watanabe, Kohli, and Agrawal 2019). The ability to get a work permit and the reduced threat of immediate deportation has made life easier for these Dreamers (so called for the proposed DREAM Act: The Development, Relief, and Education for Alien Minors Act). Most went to American public schools and experienced childhoods much like those of their neighbors who were fully documented residents or citizens. Many Dreamers do not speak the mother tongue of the country they came from. Before DACA, they were often forced to enter the low-paying jobs in the underground economy in which employers tend not to require proof of legal status.

Walter J. Nicholls (2013) writes about how remarkable it was that these young undocumented immigrants found the courage to speak up publicly and organize for their rights; it is difficult to imagine a more vulnerable group. However, they found their cause in the possibility of the DREAM Act, conceived as a way to give rights to a niche group of undocumented immigrants—these young people who were brought to this country by their parents. First introduced in the Senate in 2001, it has been reintroduced several times but never passed. Unlike DACA, which was enacted as an executive order rather than through legislation, the DREAM Act would provide a path to permanent residency and ultimately to citizenship.

Another issue the Oakland teens brought to the surface was homophobia. Clay notes that one-third of the teens who participated in her study identified as queer (2012). Just as they had the burden and the promise of past activists for the rights of black and brown students, they also had the burden and the promise of living in what has sometimes been called the "gay mecca." Teens who identified as gay often had to deal with homophobia from their peers, many of whom cited their Christian beliefs as a reason for their bias. In spite of this, the gay students seemed to be comfortable being "out" and were able to incorporate antihomophobia lessons into their anti-oppression workshops. While public libraries have contributed to a more open climate for LGBTQIA+ families by sponsoring "drag queen storytimes," for example, there isn't much literature available about what more they might be doing to support gay teens.

It is interesting to think about the causes that have generated mass movements of young people seeking to make changes in their world. Most of the children and teens who have chosen to participate in these activities are probably not consciously aware that their actions are manifestations of civic literacy. Those of us who are adult allies, however, can be more informed and sophisticated mentors and facilitators if we think about the components of civic literacy.

While most of the examples of youth activism reported in the media involve teens, younger children must certainly also think about the issues that affect them, and some seek ways to voice their concerns. In November 2019, a first grader in Takoma Park, Maryland, got the attention of local news media when she organized a protest instead of a party for her seventh birthday. Kiyoko Merolli is very opposed to the politics of President Trump, but she wanted her protest to be positive, rather than negative. Her birthday guests were invited to make picket signs promoting positive messages. They responded with signs reading "kid power," "love trumps hate," "black lives matter," and even "I like cats." Adults drove the children to the White House, where they marched with their signs and ate cupcakes. The mayor of Takoma Park, Kate Stewart, attended in support. There was no word from the office of the president as to whether or not he was aware of the demonstration (Russo 2019).

Understanding and Implementing Civic Literacy

A useful, simple definition of *civic literacy* is one provided by the Partnership for 21st Century Skills (2009, n.p.). According to their framework,

> Civic literacy is the knowledge and skills to participate effectively in civic life through knowing how to stay informed, understanding governmental processes, and knowing how to exercise the rights and obligations of citizenship at local, state, national, and global levels. Individuals also have an understanding of the local and global implications of civic decisions.

Most elementary and secondary school students are exposed to a very basic understanding of government processes, especially at a national level. Most twelve-year-olds can name the three branches of government, and many understand the different role that each play in our political system. They may also be aware that American citizens age eighteen and older can vote in elections for representatives at the local, state, and national levels. The *National Standards for Civics and Government* (Center for Civic Education 2003) outlines a compelling rationale for civic education and presents both content standards and a set of intellectual and participatory skills for students from kindergarten through twelfth grade. However, these standards, funded by the US Department of Education and the Pew Charitable Trust, are only voluntary. They are merely guidelines for schools to consider implementing. In addition to the traditional courses in government or civics, some teachers have also used literature to address issues relevant to civic literacy such as social justice and immigration. *Using Nonfiction for Civic Engagement in Classrooms* is a text intended for educator advocates using good informational literature as a way to start classroom conversations about social issues (Yenika-Agbaw, Lowery, and Ricks 2018). One of the selections in this text is about the use of nonfiction to awaken interest in the civil rights movement—an event that seems like ancient history to most contemporary students. The authors note that when middle school students finally learn about the civil rights movement, they respond with shame and guilt and become almost paralyzed into frustration and inaction (Young, Ward, and Day 2018, 15ff.). It is then up to the teacher or other adult mentor to help them see avenues for constructive action. A school or public librarian could be that adult.

There is also concern among some educators that children are not sufficiently informed about their responsibilities as citizens. Lori A. Morgan (2016) reports on the findings from Project Citizen, an evaluation study conducted on an experimental civic education curriculum implemented with a small group of middle school students. That project was developed out of a concern that young people were neither mastering the basics of civic literacy as defined by the Partnership for 21st Century Skills above, nor being motivated to learn more and exercise their civic responsibilities. The researchers concluded that it isn't enough for teens to acquire knowledge. In order to acquire needed skills, they must actually put the knowledge into practice. They must learn how to participate in civic life by doing it. Project Citizen has given them opportunities to do so; libraries can do this too.

In order to feel capable of exercising their civic responsibilities, young people must develop a belief in their individual as well as group efficacy. Civic efficacy is defined as the perceived belief someone has about their ability to participate in civic life, assume citizenship responsibilities, and make a difference (Miller 2009). In other words, children and teens need to believe in their own power to make a difference in civic life, both now and as adults. They are unlikely to develop such a belief without having firsthand evidence that they can indeed make a difference.

Findings from Morgan's report (2016) cited earlier indicate that the small group of students who participated in Project Citizen did increase their civic literacy and their sense of self-efficacy. They were particularly successful in learning how to gather information relevant to taking civic action and developing collaborative skills. However, prospects for expanding the project to greater numbers of students were not promising. There is little time in the middle or secondary school curriculum for the kind of individual and group instruction that Project Citizen requires, let alone for the opportunities to put civic knowledge into action.

Of course, classrooms are not the only place where young people acquire civic literacy. Media is an influential source of information about political life for us all. Children and teens are exposed to ever-increasing doses of digital social media. These include collaborative, peer-to-peer, and interactive platforms, which young people use to play, connect with friends, create content, and look for information for homework or everyday needs, like sports schedules or public transportation routes. They take for granted the presence of these digital media resources and often surprise others of us with their apparent mastery of them.

While even very young children appear to navigate social media platforms effortlessly, they may not be as adept at evaluating and interpreting what they find there. *Media literacy* is the term used to describe the set of skills needed to do that, and media literacy education is a means for acquiring those skills. Both the National Association for Media Literacy Education (NAMLE) and the Center for Media Literacy (CML) offer definitions, frameworks, and models for helping young people acquire those skills. NAMLE offers six core principles (Mihailidis 2014, 35):

1. Media Literacy Education requires active inquiry and critical thinking about the messages we receive and create.
2. Media Literacy Education expands the concept of literacy to include all forms of media (i.e., reading and writing).

3. Media Literacy Education builds and reinforces skills for learners of all ages. Like print literacy, those skills necessitate integrated, interactive, and repeated practice.
4. Media Literacy Education develops informed, reflective, and engaged participants essential for a democratic society.
5. Media Literacy Education recognizes that media are a part of culture and function as agents of socialization.
6. Media Literacy Education affirms that people use their individual skills, beliefs, and experiences to construct their own meanings from media messages.

While NAMLE and CML work primarily with schools seeking to develop media literacy curriculum, their websites make clear that any organizations or individuals working with a relevant constituency could be agents for advancing media literacy. In the next chapter, we will look at ways that public libraries can provide both formal and informal media literacy education along with their basic information services to young people.

Whether children and teens are acquiring civic knowledge in the classroom, from the media, by participating in voluntary activities, or from the shared opinions of adults and peers around them, this process is related to political socialization. This is the developmental process by which an individual acquires political values, ideas, attitudes, and patterns of behavior. Much of the research in this area was conducted in the late 1960s (Easton and Dennis 1969; Greenstein 1969) and drew from the work of both political science and child psychology. More recently, Robert Coles (1986) has contributed to our understanding of the child as political actor. The major findings from the research on childhood political socialization can be summarized as follows: first, children have a low interest in politics when narrowly defined to mean electoral politics and political institutions. However, at a very early age, we begin to think of ourselves as members of a politically defined community, such as Americans. By about fourth grade, we also come to understand that there is an authority other than our family that is "government." Second: children have few direct interactions with any political system or government agency. Indeed, I have often claimed that getting a library card may be a child's first civic act—and the only such act until the eighteen-year-old registers to vote. Before this age, we acquire ideas and perspectives that will later influence opinions we have about such matters as voting or immigration. Third, late childhood—the early teen years—is a critical period for the development of a person's political orientation. We may not be as politically informed in our teen years as we are later in life, but a construct of the political world is largely formed during that time.

Political efficacy is a topic relevant to both civic education and political socialization. This is an individual's belief that they are able to participate in the political system. Dennis and Easton (1969) found that by grade 3, children had begun to develop a sense of their individual political efficacy independently of their understanding of government or a citizen's role in it. There is some evidence that socioeconomic variables such as family income and education may contribute to a children's notions of their own political efficacy. However, another factor noted in my own research is participation in a youth group such as Girl Scouts or Boy Scouts. Those organizations offer children in those critical early teen years the opportunity to get involved in voluntary civic activities—visiting a nursing home, picking up litter in a park, planting trees. They acquire firsthand evidence that they could make a difference in their communities (Walter 1990). This is another obvious role for public libraries to play: we can give children and teens concrete ways to make a difference in their communities. (We will explore this further in chapter 3.)

The authors of the book *Citizens in the Present: Youth Civic Engagement in the Americas* (Torres, Rizzini, and Del Rio 2013) observed the rise in activism by young people throughout the world in 2012. They were impressed with the ways in which young people had engaged in struggles for the right to have a voice in decisions that affected them and wondered what those struggles meant for the future of democracy. They make a useful distinction between civic and political engagement, noting that children and teens are prevented from active participation in the political arena until they are old enough to vote, ordinarily at eighteen. There are, however, no barriers to their engagement in many civic activities. Young people can organize to identify and address issues that matter to them. They can organize to influence the political system. And it is important to note that they can seek out public spaces—including cyberspace—in which to exercise their collective power. The public library can be one of these spaces.

Public Libraries as Laboratories for Civic Literacy and Engagement

The American public library was founded as a cultural institution by people with an abiding respect for books and the written word. When Robert D. Leigh

(1950) looked a century back to the origins of the public library in this country, he called its ideological underpinnings the "library faith": a "belief in the virtue of the printed word, especially of the book, the reading of which is held to be good in itself or from its reading flows that which is good" (12). The idea that the mission of the public library is to collect and organize books and promote reading has remained constant. The public library has also acquired some legitimacy as an educational institution, intended to help people educate themselves and to contribute to an informed citizenry.

Redmond Kathleen Molz and Phyllis Dain (1999) have written persuasively about the social value of the traditional public library. They claim that it "anchors people to communities and fosters a sense of fellowship, civic participation, and democratic living" (2). Founded with the purpose of diffusing knowledge by providing people with books, the institution itself has evolved as the society in which it is embedded has changed. Accordingly, World War I brought new challenges and library responses, including the less desirable movement in some libraries to censor books that the US Army put on its Army Index as being too pro-German or pacifist (Wiegand 2015, 106–7). The Great Depression years saw a dramatically increased demand for books by people whose incomes had fallen or even been eliminated at the same time that library budgets were cut. Many libraries turned to federal agencies such as the National Youth Administration and the Works Progress Administration for help in staffing their branches (Wiegand 2015, 136). In Kentucky, for example, women hired by the WPA carried books on horseback to remote mountain communities.

Library historian Wayne Wiegand (2015) has documented many instances over the years in which public libraries have added a civic dimension to their primary function of providing books and reading materials. He notes that even nineteenth-century libraries had broader communal functions, including providing space for the emotional experience of community, enabling discussion groups, and at the same time cultivating a sense of freedom, status, and social privilege" (43). There are embarrassing lapses in the public library's contributions to community, of course, such as the buildings and collections that were off-limits to black people in many parts of the South, well into the twentieth century.

Librarian Ronald McCabe (2001) finds that American public libraries' commitment to a civic or social mission was eroded by an upswing in a libertarian political philosophy in the 1970s and 1980s. He laments the apparent shift in American values from community to a kind of rampant individualism and preference for utilitarianism that had infected public libraries as well as the country as a whole. He traces the origins of this approach to *A Planning Process for Public Libraries*, a 1980 publication of the Public Library Association. The planning process encouraged librarians to avoid making prescriptions about what the public library should mean and do. Instead, it encouraged them to involve the community in identifying the library's mission. While at first this sounds like a move toward engaging the library with the community, it had the effect of privileging its information role. McCabe writes, "In following the wisdom of the people and honoring individual liberty, the new institution no longer claimed to overtly educate the community, no longer claimed to prescribe specific social outcomes" (35).

Many of us who were involved in public libraries during the 1980s and 1990s remember that the new digital technologies were initially perceived as a threat to the public library as a brick-and-mortar institution—for a while, it looked like a war between books and bytes. Many progressive library leaders had a vision for the future of the institution that involved both digital and print collections. In 1996, the Benton Foundation published the results of an extensive study about public opinion of the library's future role in a digital age. Researchers found that adults did support a role for the library that combined digital and paper resources among such other traditional roles as providing reading programs for children. However, they noted that younger Americans—those between the ages of eighteen and twenty-four—were the least enthusiastic about the need to maintain public library buildings and seemed to prefer investing in their own personal computers over supporting libraries with their tax dollars. Men were also less likely than women to support any public library functions. Even frequent library users did not see libraries as leaders in the coming digital revolution (Benton Foundation 1994).

From our vantage point in the second decade of the twenty-first century, we can see that public libraries seem to have weathered the threat of obsolescence by digitization. Computers and the internet are here to stay, and libraries have staked out a role by providing access to this essential information resource. Adults still read best sellers or their preferred genre of fiction. Many people still need help finding the right search term to yield an answer to their question as they sit in front of their home computers. Librarians are there to help. And increasingly, public librarians are seeing ways that they can help their neighbors solve problems that impact their communities. They have become active partners with other community agencies and individuals working to improve the lives of the people they serve.

Library literature is full of references to public library partnerships with organizations. Many of these received at least initial funding from grants; of course, not all have been sustained. A publication from the California State Library (Francisco et al. 2001) describes seventeen different projects that exemplify various kinds of partnerships. The initiative Adelante! Developing a Healthy Reading Habit was implemented through a partnership between the Oceanside Public Library and the San Diego County Health and Human Services Agency's Public Health Department to use modified catering trucks as bookmobiles in low-income Latinx communities. These trucks—staffed by public health nurses as well as librarians—distributed information instead of ice cream. The book also describes partnerships with major sports organizations, small family foundations, cable television and other media, and the chamber of commerce. What all these partnership initiatives have in common is an expansion of the library's traditional role beyond books or bytes and into significant civic relationships.

Recent trends in public libraries indicate a renewed interest in fostering those civic relationships. If there is any doubt that public library leaders see civic engagement as an important emerging role, the July/August 2019 issue of *Public Libraries* should put that to rest. This is a special issue devoted to "Civic Engagement." It is tempting to report on all the projects highlighted in the issue, and I urge you to check it out if you can. Here are a few projects worth thinking about: The nonprofit organization Hispanic Unity of Florida holds citizenship classes in more than ten branches of the Broward County Public Library (Riggs 2019). Many libraries are offering community forums as ways to involve people in conversations about civic issues that affect them. Sno-Isle Libraries in Washington has been holding forums on the theme "Issues That Matter" for more than ten years. These sessions include panelists and a program moderator and are streamed live on Facebook. Among the first topics covered were controversial state ballot measures: a tax measure, legalization of recreational marijuana, and same-sex marriage. More recently, homelessness has become an important issue, and that forum in 2017 had the most participation of any Issues That Matter event. Sno-Isle librarians involved with these forums note that they have created enormously useful partnerships between the various panelists who have participated and the agencies where they work. People who attend seem appreciative, finding that the forums are informative and help bring people together (Pratt, Gustafson, and Batdorf 2019).

The Civic Lab at the Skokie Public Library in Illinois is upfront about its aim to connect people in its community with the information and resources they need to understand issues impacting their community, to form opinions about them, and determine whether and how to act as a result. It started with a "Civic Lab Boutique" in a corner of its AV department. The Civic Lab focused on six issues that were important in Skokie at the time: the Black Lives Matter movement, climate change, immigration, income inequality, LGBTQIA+ rights, and reproductive justice. For each issue, the Civic Lab included small curated collections (two resources for adults, two for teens, and one for middle grade students, plus one picture book), conversation starters, voting prompts, and handouts giving further resources. Beginning in 2016, the library introduced Civic Lab pop-ups. They involve the same elements as the Civic Lab Boutique, with the addition of staffing and a whiteboard with dry-erase markers to facilitate participant sharing. They offer at least one pop-up topic each month. Over time, they have learned some best practices for this kind of civic information effort. They avoid an "opposing viewpoints" model—they believe there are often more than two sides to a complex issue. They have learned that children are drawn to activities they see as fun, rather than as purely educational or informational. Teens tend to get engaged with topics that feel personally relevant to them. Adults look to have civic conversations in which they are both respected and intellectually stimulated (Koester 2019).

The Skokie Civic Lab is a model that is remarkable in many ways, not least for the way in which it involves children and teens as well as adults. Of course, the earliest public libraries did not open their doors to children and teens, much less try to inculcate values of civic literacy and engagement in young people. It wasn't until the end of the nineteenth century that pioneering librarians began to develop specialized services and spaces for children. Libraries flourished after this, with the Carnegie library movement contributing to their growth. All Carnegie libraries included space for a children's room. Pioneering children's librarians such as Anne Carroll Moore, Frances Jenkins Olcott, and Mary Wright Plummer were passionate believers in the library faith as it applied to children. They all advocated for the best in literature for the young people who entered their library doors.

That belief in the power of books and reading was also present in the origins of library services for teens. Mabel Williams was head of the School Work Department at the New York Public Library in 1919 (Braverman 1979). Margaret Edwards (1974) was hired to develop teen services at the Enoch Pratt Free

Library in Baltimore in 1933, and Amelia Munson wrote the first manual for young adult services, *An Ample Field*, in 1950. Books and reading were still at the heart of the service they were pioneering.

Library youth services were not immune to changes in the world outside their doors, and this led to some expansion of the traditional focus on reading. During the Great Depression, for example, Edwards launched a campaign to make the promotion of world citizenship a core value of young adult services (Wiegand 2015, 143). Still, as Miriam Braverman (1979) writes in her overview of public library youth services, the intent was always reading promotion in some form. She profiles the work of three public library systems noted for an early embrace of specialized service to teens—New York Public Library, Cleveland Public Library, and Enoch Pratt Library in Baltimore. While all these libraries mounted programs involving film showings, discussions, exhibits, and author visits, these efforts were aimed at increasing teens' reading. In fact, some young adult librarians worried that their programs did nothing to increase circulation, and when budgets and staffing levels were tight in the mid-1950s, programs were cut as a result (Braverman 1979).

Braverman reports one interesting exception to the nearly universal emphasis on book-related programming. In 1948, two branches of the Enoch Pratt Public Library launched a Civic Experience Project in partnership with a local high school. For five years, students from the high school and the two branch libraries worked on a "social resource map" of their neighborhood. The teens suggested ways that the library could advance its objectives in the community through orientation, observation, and participation. They then worked with library staff to accomplish those objectives (Braverman 1979, 207).

Rather than sift through the annals of library history for more examples of public library initiatives to contribute to the civic literacy of children and teens, let's turn to more recent manifestations. One landmark in changing the conversation among young adult librarians is Public Libraries as Partners in Youth Development (PLPYD), a project funded by the DeWitt Wallace–Reader's Digest Fund in 1998. This initiative was intended to help public libraries develop quality activities and programs that support the educational and career needs of young people in out-of-school hours. It put youth-development outcomes at the center of this work. Ten public library systems throughout the country participated in this effort to find and test strategies to engage teens more deeply and fully (Simone 1999).

One of the operating principles that became a kind of key phrase from the PLPYD project was "work with, not for" teens. This represented a sea change in philosophy about the relationship between the professional librarian and the teenager. The librarian would no longer proceed as if they knew what was best and appropriate to offer teens in the way of books, digital resources, and program opportunities. Instead they would engage the teen as a partner in making most of those decisions. Youth advisory boards, one of the ways in which this approach was implemented, have now become commonplace in libraries that have a youth services specialist on staff, as well as in many others that are less well staffed. (We will look more closely at this opportunity for youth engagement in chapter 3.)

Just as *Public Libraries* focused on civic engagement with a special issue in July/August 2019, *Young Adult Library Services*, the official journal of the Young Adult Library Services Association, devoted its Winter 2018 issue to youth activism. Articles included reports of best practices around the country as well as a roundup of relevant research. (Look for more discussion of these initiatives in chapter 3 as well.)

There has been little emphasis on participation and activism in library services for children. This is probably due at least in part to a lack of emphasis on civic engagement in traditional child development philosophy and practice. However, some of the theory and research about children's rights points to a rationale for integrating opportunities for participation and engagement into our library work with children. This too will be discussed in chapters 2 and 3.

Here we have explored a literature review and framework for thinking about the public library's role in cultivating civic literacy and engagement in children and teens. The next two chapters will go into detail with ideas and strategies for doing this. We will look first at the civic literacy mandate to be informed—which the public library plays a natural role in supporting. Then we will explore ways that the public library can help children and teens specifically exercise their rights and obligations as active participants in civic engagement.

CHAPTER 2

Information for Young Activists

s defined in chapter 1, civic literacy requires that people have the information they need to identify and understand civic issues and their rights, as well as the mechanisms to address all of these. In this chapter, we will look at strategies that libraries can use to leverage their traditional role as information provider to better equip children and teens with the knowledge and resources to participate fully as active agents for change. First we will look at the kinds of civic information libraries can make available. We will then look at strategies for getting that information into the hearts, hands, and minds of children and teens.

Teens, Children, and Civic Information

What resources would best meet the civic information needs of young people? The report *National Standards for Civics and Government* (Center for Civic Education 2003) mentioned in chapter 1 provides some guidance on the kinds of information middle and high school students might seek out to satisfy homework demands—information that many public libraries continue to provide. Schools that integrate these standards into middle school curricula would be teaching basic concepts of civic life, politics, and government. Students are asked to think about *why* we need government and to understand some fundamental ideas about our political culture and the values and principles that underly American constitutional democracy, such as the rule of law. The rights and responsibilities of citizens are also introduced.

Secondary school curricula based on the *Standards* would continue the exploration of these topics with more nuanced and increasingly sophisticated treatment. For example, in grades 5 to 8, students are expected to be able to evaluate, take, and defend positions on the influence of the media on American political life. They should be able to evaluate information and arguments received from various sources in order to make reasonable choices on public issues and among candidates for political office (Center for Civic Education 2003, 69). In high school, students look more closely at contemporary political communication using criteria such as logical validity, factual accuracy, emotional appeal, distorted evidence, and appeals to bias. They may study wartime propaganda and political cartoons (119).

How can the public library support this curriculum? After all, we are not classroom teachers. We are not responsible for what students learn in school or what assignments they are given. We can, however, take homework-related inquiries seriously and provide the best possible information in response to those requests. Melissa Gross (1995) has contributed to our understanding of the nature of these kinds of reference questions through her research on imposed queries. These are not self-generated questions but rather questions that a teacher has directed students to answer. The student may have a different interpretation of the question or topic than the teacher had in assigning it. This leads to potential difficulties for the librarian who is trying to assist the student. As Gross notes, the librarian must work backward with the student to try to figure out what the teacher really intended when identifying the right resource to meet this imposed information need.

Assuming that the librarian and the student have arrived at an understanding of what information is required, the librarian can steer students toward reputable print and online sources. We can also take the initiative to inculcate some information literacy guidance at the same time. Students are most likely to encounter fake news online. Why not post warnings or reminders of this next to the public access computers? Or make a simple handout for teens to keep in their notebooks or backpacks. The Stanford History Education Group (n.d.,) has a downloadable poster that reminds students to evaluate information online by asking the following questions:

- Who's behind the information?
- What's the evidence?
- What do other sources say?

The National Association for Media Literacy Education (NAMLE, n.d.) also has a downloadable one-page poster with tips for becoming a critical thinker, an effective communicator, and an engaged citizen. The poster advises information seekers to ask the following questions as they encounter messages in all media:

- WHO made this?
- WHY was it made?
- WHAT is missing from this message?
- HOW might different people interpret this message?
- WHO might benefit from this message?
- WHO might be harmed by this message?

You can also remind teens to be suspicious of URLs that end in *.co* or *.su* and to consult fact-checking websites such as Snopes.com to see if the story has already been debunked or if the site is a known provider of hoax information.

Paul Mihailidis has developed a quick model of media literacy that is geared particularly to teens, whom he calls "emerging citizens" (2014, 128). The 5 A's of Media Literacy in this model are:

1. Access to media.
2. Awareness of authority, context, credibility.
3. Assessment of how media portray events and issues.
4. Appreciation for the diversity of information, dialog, collaboration, and voices online.
5. Action to become part of the dialog.

These points would make good discussion starters with your teen advisory board about a possible media literacy campaign or series of programs that the library might sponsor. The teens themselves could be resource people for a library-based media literacy initiative, advising on the social media currently being used by their peers.

Less sophisticated teens may be particularly vulnerable to "clickbait"— the online practice of using shocking or teasing headlines to trick the user into clicking a link for more information. The purpose of clickbait is often to increase social media sharing for commercial or political purposes. Librarians can remind patrons, and teens and children in particular, to be suspicious of sensational headlines. Teens may also need to learn about satirical online sources such as the *Onion* (http://theonion.com/).

All these aspects of media literacy would be good topics for teen advisory boards to consider. Teens would have good ideas for promoting positive media literacy practices among their peers. Would teens in your community bother to read your posters or bookmarks listing good media literacy practices? Would they respond better to messages created by teens themselves? Would they be interested in hearing directly from other teens? What kinds of examples of biased messages would resonate with them?

Elementary school children are probably not getting the same level of civic education as secondary students are. However, they are exposed to much of the same political and civic discourse through media and through adult influence. They are aware when national elections are being held. They are probably aware of the hot-button topics in their families and communities, whether they are immigration, gun control, climate change, or discrimination of any kind. They may not formulate questions at the reference desk, but they are open to receiving information in other ways.

Creating an Open Information Environment

Part of our code of professional ethics is the requirement that we be value-neutral in our presentation of information. I have always interpreted this to mean that we do not pass judgment on the information requests we receive. The classic example from library school was Zoia Horn, the Bucknell University librarian who went to jail for contempt of court when she refused to testify against antiwar activists. It is relatively easy to build a collection that reflects various viewpoints on controversial topics—for instance, abortion—without actually presenting content that is untrue. Some topics are a little trickier than others. As I write this book, even a topic like "fake news" is problematic, with the president and the leaders of his political party accusing reputable news media of being purveyors of such news. We want to create an environment in our libraries that encourages young people to look for answers to tough questions, to expand their knowledge of the world, and to nurture their curiosity about all things.

One way to do this is through bulletin board displays. Get feedback from children and teens about the issues and topics that concern them. I guarantee that climate change will be one of them. Other topics might reflect more local concerns: school safety or immigration issues. Then ask for teens' help in creating a bulletin board or display case that features that topic. It could include banners or posters with provocative questions aligned with resources that address those queries:

- What are my rights if ICE knocks on our door?
- What can we do to make our school safe?
- What can a kid do for the environment?

Consider putting up a "free speech" bulletin board in your YA area. Encourage teens to post their thoughts on any current issues: #MeToo, #BlackLives Matter, or anything else that comes to mind. You could make this a totally open forum for any topic related to civic engagement and social issues or make it a rotating forum with a focus on a specific topic. Perhaps your teen advisory board (TAB) members or other interested teens could be in charge of monitoring the board for inappropriate messages or hate speech. Be sure to provide paper, pens, and pushpins. Making a whiteboard or blackboard available for thoughts and slogans following a program about a current issue is another idea. The moderator could invite attendees to share their immediate thoughts on the board and then talk about them.

Public forums might be a welcome alternative in many communities to more traditional teen fare such as movie nights. The Harwood Institute for Public Innovation has partnered with the American Library Association to train librarians around the country in the holding community conversations as part of the initiative Libraries Transforming Communities. These conversations are intended to help public libraries engage meaningfully with the people in their communities and to generate what they refer to as public knowledge. This is a way to identify key issues, generate a sense of common purpose, and lead to better decisions. The *Community Conversations Workbook* (ALA and Harwood Institute, n.d.) is an excellent guide to planning, holding, and following up on a series of community conversations. While there is nothing in the workbook that suggests restricting attendance to adults, the section on deciding whom to invite suggests staff, volunteers, and board members as well as agencies that partner with the library. Check out the workbook, share it with your TAB, and consider how you could hold community conversations with teens and even children.

Booktalks as Sources of Civic Information

Providing ethical, professional assistance to teens at the reference desk and enlisting their help in promoting media literacy are just two ways to create an open information environment in our libraries. There are other ways that we can do this, for children as well as for teens. We can use our bulletin boards and display cases to highlight civic issues. We can include civic content in the booktalks we give to promote the use of our print collections, and we can create booklists that highlight relevant resources about hot topics and pertinent issues. These make students aware that the library has resources about real-world matters and may their spark curiosity to learn more.

Let's consider booktalks first. Young adult and children's librarians have been promoting books by talking about them to groups for decades. Joni Bodart (1993) was the pied piper who popularized this strategy through articles in the library press and some practical books that are still in print. Librarians typically introduce booktalks to classes who visit the library or on visits to classrooms in schools. I suggest that we can be more creative in our thinking about potential audiences for booktalks. What about visits to or from the local Boys & Girls Club? Meetings of library teen volunteers or Junior Friends of the Library? Adult groups such as parents or teachers? Most of the booktalks suggested below could be adapted to introduce books on a relevant topic to adults who are looking for books to share with young.

Sample Booktalks*

LEADING TEENS FROM VOLUNTARISM TO ACTIVISM
Audience: Meeting of library teen volunteers

I just read a book that made me think of you. You have already shown your commitment to making your community a better place by volunteering to help out at the library. Maybe some of you would like to take that commitment a step further and do even more. This book would give you a lot of strategies for doing that. It's called *You Are Mighty: A Guide to Changing the World* by Caroline Paul. This book doesn't tell you which cause or issue to support or try to change. It just gives you many ideas for going about it. There's advice for everything from making an effective protest sign to writing letters that get attention to marching, boycotting, and walking out. The writing style is casual but informative, and the illustrations are appealing. You can do this! Read this book and change the world. You could even share it with your younger brothers and sisters; its message is accessible to a wide range of ages. You might also be interested in another book, *Online Activism: Social Change through Social Media* by Amanda Vink. Your generation uses social media like no other before it; read this one to find out how you can make those digital connections work for social change.

CLIMATE CHANGE
Audience: Grade 8 or 9

I get why young people like you are worried about the environment, especially the warming climate. Your lives are already being dramatically impacted. Here is a novel—*Dry* by Neal Shusterman—that looks at a fictional future California that has been experiencing a severe drought for a long time. Now the taps have run completely dry. Sixteen-year-old Alyssa's parents have gone to look for water and haven't returned. Alyssa, her little brother, and the teenage son of the survivalist family next door set off to find her parents. They meet up with other teens and negotiate their way through an increasingly violent world in which people are beginning to die from lack of water. This is a kind of nightmare scenario, but it will definitely make you think—and probably want to get involved

*All the titles suggested here and in the following section on storytimes are listed with bibliographic information and annotations in the last chapter of this book that focuses on resources.

to make sure things don't reach this point. Here are a few nonfiction titles that will give you more information about climate change and some ideas for turning it around: *No One Is Too Small to Make a Difference* by Greta Thunberg, the young Swedish activist, is a compilation of her speeches and writings on this subject; if you need more information and evidence that global warming is real and what you can do about it, take a look at *Gaia Warriors* by Nicola Davies or *Earth in the Hot Seat* by Marfe Ferguson Delano and many other books in our collection that I can point you to.

MUHAMMAD ALI AND OTHER MALE ACTIVISTS
Audience: Grade 4 or 5

How many of you have heard of the boxer Muhammad Ali? He was already a famous boxing champion when he was drafted into the army in 1967. He refused to go into the army because of his religious beliefs and his opposition to the Vietnam War. He was threatened with jail, and his passport was taken away. After three years of speaking out about his opposition to the war and the struggle of other African Americans, the United States Supreme Court ruled that he could not be jailed for his resistance to the draft on religious grounds. You can read more about that episode in his life in this book by Tonya Bolden: *The Champ: The Story of Muhammad Ali.* You might also like *Twelve Rounds to Glory: The Story of Muhammad Ali* by Charles R. Smith. It tells about his life in the style of rap. You can read more about other peace activists in *Paths to Peace: People Who Changed the World* by Jane Breskin Zalben. *Groundbreaking Guys: 40 Men Who Became Great by Doing Good* by Stephanie True Peters is full of stories about celebrities like Kareem Abdul-Jabbar and Kendrick Lamar and other, less familiar men who contributed to the good of the world. Maybe someday we'll be reading about the good work that one of you is doing to make the world a better place.

TREES AND ENVIRONMENTAL ACTIVISM
Audience: Grade 2 or 3

Have you ever stopped and really looked at a tree? Maybe one in your yard or one that you see at the park or on your way to school? Trees are not just beautiful; they are also useful. Here are two books—*Tell Me, Tree* by Gail Gibbons and *A Tree Is a Plant* by Clyde Bulla—that will give you a lot of general information about trees. Trees are important not just here, where you live, but all around the world. *Who Will Plant a Tree?* by Jerry Pallotta is a book about trees all around the globe. Trees are important for so many reasons. You can read *How the Ladies Stopped the Wind* by Bruce McMillan to see why some old ladies in Iceland planted trees to stop the fierce winds that blow in their country. And finally, here is one of my favorite books: *Seeds of Change* by Jen Cullerton Johnson. It tells the story of Wangari Maathai, a Kenyan woman who decided to do something about the terrible damage that had been done to her country when so many trees were cut down. She started a campaign of tree planting. It was mostly women who got involved, and they planted more than thirty million trees! She was so successful that she attracted the attention of some powerful businessmen who bribed corrupt police officers to arrest her. The good news is that she was finally released from jail and went on to win the Nobel Peace Prize in 2004.

CIVIL RIGHTS MOVEMENT
Audience: Grades 6–8
Christopher Paul Curtis is one of my favorite authors of books for young people. Some of you might have read *Bud, Not Buddy*. He got the Newbery Medal for that one, and it's a really good book. My favorite, though, is *The Watsons Go to Birmingham—1963*. Ten-year-old Kenny tells the story about his family's trip from Flint, Michigan, to Birmingham, Alabama, in 1963. It's a funny story until right at the end. It's Sunday morning. The family is staying at Kenny's grandma's house. Little sister Joetta has already gone to Sunday school. There is a huge boom. The church has been bombed. Read this book to find out what happened and how Kenny responds. And if you want to know more about what happened in Birmingham that day in 1963 and in the early days of the civil rights movement, here are just a few of the great books about this topic you can find at the library:

- *A Dream of Freedom: The Civil Rights Movement from 1954 to 1968* by Diane McWhorter
- *When the Children Marched: The Birmingham Civil Rights Movement* by Robert H. Mayer
- *Witness to Freedom: Young People Who Fight for Civil Rights* by Belinda Rochelle

SUPERHEROES IN FANTASY AND REAL LIFE
Audience: Grades 5–7

Do you ever wish you had superpowers? Then you could be a really good activist, changing the world for the better, right? Maybe you've read some of the books about Percy Jackson, a kid who's a demigod because his father was Poseidon, the god of the sea. The first book was *The Sea of Monsters*, and there have been more since then. They are all great adventure stories in which Percy and his friends tackle injustice and prevail. Of course, Percy Jackson had the help of his father and other Roman gods. There are many gods in the mythology of other cultures, and you can read about kids who carry their genes in a new series presented by Rick Riordan. In *The Storm Runner* by J. C. Cervantes, Zane Obispo learned that he is the son of the Mayan god Hurakan, and that he must kill the evil god Ah-Puch or the world will be destroyed. And Tristan Strong is an ordinary seventh grader until a stay at his grandparents' home in Alabama leads him to a magical collaboration with Brer Rabbit, John Henry, and finally Anansi. Together, they must mend a rip in the sky before the world ends. Min looks like an ordinary Korean girl, but she is really a fox spirit living in a future world where her brother is part of the Space Forces. In this story, she joins him on a dangerous quest for the Dragon Pearl. Read about it in *Dragon Pearl* by Yoon Ha Lee. And Aru Shah was living an ordinary life until she lights the Lamp of Bharata at the museum where her mother works and frees the Sleeper, a demon whose mission is to awaken the Hindu god of destruction. Only Aru can stop him. Roshani Chokshi has told this story in *Aru Shah and the End of Time*.

But these are not ordinary kids. They are endowed with supernatural powers and special relationships to mythological gods. What can ordinary kids like you do? Marley Dias was a sixth-grade girl who loved to read but couldn't find enough books about black girls like her. So she started the #1000blackgirlbooks campaign to locate 1,000 books about black girls, collect them, and distribute them to children. Her social media skills and charismatic personality attracted celebrity supporters like Hillary Clinton, Ellen DeGeneres, and director Ava DuVernay. She wrote a book called *Marley Dias Gets It Done and So Can You!* You have probably heard about Malala Yousafzai, the Pakistani teenager who was shot while on a bus to school for her efforts on behalf of education for girls in her country. She won the Nobel Peace Prize for those efforts. You may not be as familiar with Iqbal, a boy who spent hours every day chained to a loom until he managed to get free. He then worked tirelessly to end child labor in his country, until like Malala, he was shot. Unlike Malala, he did not survive; but his campaign lived on after his death. You can read about both of these young heroes in a book by Jeannette Winter, *Malala, a Brave Girl from Pakistan/Iqbal, a Brave Boy from Pakistan: Two Stories of Bravery*.

As Marley would say, "Imagine, believe, achieve."

ANTIWAR ACTIVISM
Audience: Grades 7–9

Your grandparents might have been young during the Vietnam War, which lasted from the early 1960s until 1975. You should ask them about it. Those were turbulent times in this country. Young men were being drafted into the army, and some fled to Canada in order to avoid fighting a war they didn't believe in. Those who gained conscientious objector status sometimes served in alternate ways—in hospitals, for example. *Vietnam: A History of the War* by Russell Freedman is a readable account of the events leading up to that war, how America got involved, and the aftermath. It also includes a good chapter on the antiwar movement that was led largely by young activists. *Boots on the Ground* by Elizabeth Partridge is another good nonfiction book that presents many aspects of the Vietnam War from the perspective of individual soldiers who fought it, politicians who supported it, and some people who opposed it, including Dr. Martin Luther King Jr. and singer Country Joe McDonald. One book that focuses on the antiwar movement is *Stop This War!* by Margot Fortunato Galt.

Some celebrities got involved as well, including Muhammad Ali. To learn more about his role, read *Twelve Rounds to Glory: The Story of Muhammad Ali* by Charles Smith. Feelings were strong, whether people were for or against the war. Sometimes a novel can tell us more than nonfiction can about the experiences of ordinary people caught in a big historical event. Read *Letters from Wolfie* by Patti Sherlock to learn how one American family's life was disrupted by the Vietnam War. One son volunteers to fight; his younger brother donates his German shepherd dog to be trained as a scout. The father supports the war; the mother does not. And when the older son returns from Vietnam with his leg amputated at the knee and now totally opposed to the war, the family must cope with many conflicting feelings. Another novel—one that depicts the less heroic aspects of the Vietnam War—is *Shooting the Moon* by Frances O'Roark Dowell. Twelve-year-old Jamie is thrilled when her big brother goes to Vietnam to fight. However, instead of letters describing the excitement of combat, she receives rolls of undeveloped film that depict incidents of brutality. What can a little sister do?

Encouraging Activism through Storytelling

Booktalks are a traditional way for librarians to introduce children to resources to read for pleasure and information. We always hope that those two purposes will coexist. Librarians also read and tell stories for audiences that range from babies sitting in laps to toddlers and preschoolers to multigeneration family groups. These may be tellings of a single story as part of a class visit, or a more formal storytime that involves several picture books and maybe a finger play or flannel board story as well. Storytimes that feature traditional folktales told without a book are less common these days, but those librarians who still carry on this art can testify to its power and appeal. What follows are several storytime programs that highlight themes related to activism.

TREES AND ENVIRONMENTAL ACTIVISM
Audience: Preschool storytime (3- and 4-year-olds)
These stories are good for an autumn storytime when leaves are changing color.

Books
- *The Busy Tree* by Jennifer Ward
- *Caps for Sale* by Esphyr Slobodkina
- *Leaf Jumpers* by Carole Gerber
- *Red Leaf, Yellow Leaf* by Lois Ehlert
- *A Tree Is Nice* by Janice May Udry

Nursery rhyme/song/movement activity
- "Here We Go Round the Mulberry Bush"
- Ask children (and parents, if they are present) if they can think of any other songs or nursery rhymes about trees. This often helps parents remember rhymes from their own childhoods, which is especially interesting if they grew up in another country with another language.

STORIES FOR "WOKE" CHILDREN AND THEIR PARENTS
Audience: Family storytime

Books
- *A Is for Activist* by Innosanto Nagara
- *Julian Is a Mermaid* by Jessica Love
- *Last Stop on Market Street* by Matt de la Pena
- *We March* by Shane Evans
- *What Can a Citizen Do?* by Dave Eggers

Songs
- "This Little Light of Mine"

CLIMATE CHANGE
Audience: Family storytime

Books
- *Earth Feeling the Heat* by Brenda Z. Guiberson
- *The Magic School Bus and the Climate Challenge* by Joanna Cole and Bruce Degen
- *Why Are the Ice Caps Melting?* by Anne E. Rockwell

It would also be fun to share a couple of picture books that remind us of the pleasures we get from the weather we have and the many reasons to avert the negative consequences of global warming. Some possibilities include:

- *Rain!* by Linda Ashman
- *Sally Goes to the Beach* by Stephen Huneck
- *The Snowy Day* by Ezra Jack Keats

Activity
Share the ideas for getting involved found in *True Green Kids: 100 Things Kids Can Do to Save the Planet* by Kim McKay and Jenny Bonnin, and *Kids Care! 75 Ways to Make a Difference for People, Animals, and the Environment* by Rebecca Olien.

More Ways to Use Folktales

In addition to presenting storytime programs, librarians can weave single tales—picture books or traditional stories told without a book—into many occasions. These can be impromptu stories told to a group of restless kids waiting to be picked up at the library after school or as part of a presentation about the services of the library to adults. Trickster tales are particularly good introductions to the notion of civic engagement and activism because they typically feature a small, weak creature getting the best of a bigger, stronger creature. Here are a few of my favorites. You can use them in many different ways—I leave that up to you.

- *Anansi the Spider: A Tale from the Ashanti* by Gerald McDermott (See also many other trickster tales by McDermott, such as *Monkey: A Trickster Tale from India* and *Raven: A Trickster Tale from the Pacific Northwest.*)
- *Borreguita and the Coyote* by Verna Aardema
- *Bruh Rabbit and the Tar Baby Girl* by Virginia Hamilton
- *Conejito* by Margaret MacDonald
- *Jack Outwits the Giants* by Paul Brett Johnson
- *Just a Minute: A Trickster Tale and Counting Book* by Yuyi Morales
- *The Tale of Rabbit and Coyote* by Tony Johnson

Margaret Read MacDonald has collected many stories that are relevant to social justice and activism. I have included two of these collections in chapter 4, under the heading "Adult Resources." Librarians who do traditional storytelling probably already have a repertoire of tales that would be appropriate. For example, *The Hat-Shaking Dance* by Harold Courlander includes many Anansi trickster tales, all well-honed for oral telling. Judy Sierra is another storyteller who has published compilations of very tellable tales. *Can You Guess My Name?* contains many stories in which the small and the weak outwit the large and the powerful.

It might seem as though I am suggesting that *all* children's and young adult programming be focused on issues related to civic engagement and activism. That is not my intent. Obviously there will always be a need for library programs that are purely cultural or entertaining. However, it would be a shame to pass up the chance to shine a light on issues that matter to young people and their families. Watch for holidays or current events that are natural occasions for encouraging the active involvement of children and teens. Think about making the public library a space where young people expect to find information and opportunities that enable them to work for a better world. In the next chapter, we will explore ways that the library can put civic literacy into action through various forms of civic engagement.

CHAPTER 3

Putting Civic Literacy to Work

Engaging Children and Teens as Active Participants in Their Communities

n chapter 1, we introduced the notion that civic literacy has two components. It requires having information about one's rights and obligations as well as about issues relevant to social change and justice. It also requires knowing how to exercise those rights and obligations. Abstract knowledge isn't enough; civic literacy requires practice in putting those rights and obligation into action. This chapter focuses on ways that public libraries can provide children and teens with practice in civic engagement. Some of these are well-established programs found in almost all public libraries, such as teen advisory boards and volunteer opportunities. Others are exciting new programs found in some pioneering libraries, such as Teens Leading Change at Los Angeles Public Library. And others are ideas waiting to be implemented by librarians who are also advocates for child and teen activists.

Before considering specific strategies for engaging children and teens more actively in the mission of our libraries, it is useful to look at a model for youth participation. Consider this "ladder of participation" developed by Dr. Roger Hart at the City University of New York:

Degrees of participation

8. Child-initiated, shared decisions with adults.

7. Child-initiated and directed.

6. Adult-initiated, shared decisions with children.

5. Consulted and informed.

4. Assigned but informed.

Non-participation

3. Tokenism.

2. Decoration.

1. Manipulation.

Adapted from: Hart, Roger. (1992). *Children's Participation from Tokenism to Citizenship.* Florence: UNICEF Innocenti Research Center.

Diane Tuccillo (2010) provides a good discussion of the ladder of youth participation as it applies to library services. She notes that examples of initiatives at level 8 are rare but worthy of aspiration. Even activities at the lowest level of the scale confer a benefit to teens. For example, those asked to help out at a friend's book sale often get credit for community service at their school and also have the experience of working with adults on a worthwhile project. But she urges librarians to avoid the practices at the nonparticipation level of the scale, which only disrespect young people and devalue their efforts, and might lead children and teens to distrust all opportunities for engagement, even beyond the library.

Teen Advisory Boards

Let's start by taking a good look at youth participation through library advisory boards. Teen advisory boards (TABs) have become a standard example of a "best practice" in young adult library services. They can be organized in a number of ways. Some TABs are very informal, with small groups of interested teens meeting to suggest ideas for book purchases or programs. Others are highly formalized, with membership rolls and elected officers. Some function as junior Friends of the Library. Diane P. Tuccillo, author of the practical book *Teen-Centered Library Services: Putting Youth Participation into Practice* (2010), suggests that TAB participation is best defined as a volunteer activity. This makes TABs less vulnerable to cuts during tight budget times; it also makes it possible to cover the teens under the liability insurance that many libraries offer to their volunteers.

Library systems have several options for organizing their TABs. They may have one TAB that advises the system as a whole, or they may sponsor individual TABs at each branch. The Santa Cruz (CA) Public Library has two teen advisory groups. Their Teen Advisory Council is based at a single location—the system's branch that is dedicated to young adult services. Their Advisory Council of Teens includes members from each of the ten library branches and rotates meetings among its three larger facilities.

TABs also vary in their mission and activities, as well as where their operations stand on the "ladder of participation" above. Some exist solely to advise YA librarians on issues relating to collection development and programming. Others are actively involved in programming—planning and implementing events like teen job fairs and author visits. Some TABs are involved in fundraising—sponsoring events like book fairs and bake sales. Others focus on volunteering for various library services. (The next section deals more specifically with this function.) However the TAB is organized and whatever activities it decides to mount, it is important that the staff give them space and resources to work independently. As in all aspects of young adult library service, it is important to remember to work *with*, not *for*, the teens.

I talked with four young women from the West Covina branch of the Los Angeles County Library System. Two were in high school, one was in middle school, and the fourth was a college student who was still interested in the work the library does for teens (she comes back to visit and help when she can). This informal scaffolding of young people of different ages provides a natural form of leadership development and continuity. The volunteers were proud of the work they did, which they saw as benefiting both the library and other teens. Their primary work with the TAB was planning events. One said, "We try to create programs that are intriguing." The volunteers said that anything with food was successful, and they were still talking about a program that challenged participants to "guess this chocolate." Another program that they were proud of was about choosing a career and applying for a job.

These teens from West Covina also felt that they had personally benefited from their work with TAB. Brianna, the high school graduate who had stayed involved with the library's teen program, said that she was from a low-income family with no internet access at home. Nobody in her family had gone to college before her. She said that she learned about the college application process at the library. Ernest, the young adult librarian, had steered her to reliable information about colleges and had written a recommendation for her.

Ernest encouraged the TAB members to be ambassadors to children and other teens in the community. He said that the teens were often more approachable to kids than the adult staff were. The TAB members played a significant role in recruiting community members to join the summer reading program and telling other young people about the library's resources. Ruby, a seventh grader, talked about how Ernest encouraged her to approach an adult about an upcoming program: "He told me to just go up to this person and talk. So I did it."

Teens Leading Change is an initiative of the Los Angeles Public Library, funded by its library foundation. Mini grants of $100 to $5,000 are given to projects developed by the library's Teen Councils to projects related to:

- library advocacy and information literacy
- cultural/community conversations and archives
- knowing your rights, immigration, and citizenship
- net neutrality/privacy
- voting rights and registration

The first cycles produced some extraordinary projects, including Community by Design at Pacoima Branch Library, in which the teens visited eleven local museums and galleries that featured Latinx artists and then worked with a local muralist and the neighborhood council to design and paint a community mural. Teens at Cypress Park Branch Library developed skills to combat illegal evictions and creeping gentrification in their neighborhood. The group Westwood Teens partnered with the City of Los Angeles Department of Aging to learn more about senior rights and to help seniors learn how to use LAPL e-media resources. The Past Is Our FUTURE is a project of the Little Tokyo Branch to gather oral history and testimonies from older residents, produce manga books based on those stories, and contribute to an ongoing archive.

Volunteer Opportunities

Being part of a TAB led the girls from West Covina to many other volunteer opportunities, most of which involved communicating with other people. Like so many teens I have talked with about their voluntarism, these girls confessed to being shy at first. Like Ruby, they had to be pushed to talk to strangers. They said that Ernest was always respectful and considerate when he gave them feedback. They remembered how he helped them develop successful marketing approaches when they sold candy during Friends of the Library book sales.

Araceli said, "The more I volunteer, the more I grow and feel confident talking to adults. You don't just help other people, but you help yourself."

Ernest offered a few other keys to working effectively with teen volunteers. He tried to make every teen feel accepted. Personal relationships are important and require a kind of balance between being a friend and serving as a supervisor. He said that he can be a friend, but he can't cross the line into a relationship that is too informal. He said it sometimes take persistence to win a teen's trust and confidence, but it's worth it when it happens. For Ernest, the most fulfilling part of the job is seeing teens succeed. He talked about the local high school valedictorian who was admitted to Harvard. In her high school graduation speech, she thanked Ernest for the help he had given her.

The teen volunteers at the West Covina Library started their engagement with the library on the teen advisory board. Through the TAB they were drawn into volunteer roles. At the Vista Library in San Diego County, there is a veritable army of teens who volunteer throughout the year—often more than one hundred at a given time. They did not start out as advisory board members. Instead, they jumped right into volunteering in other areas. Summertime is the peak season for their involvement in the library; most of the teens are not in school then, and the library runs a big summer lunch program. This makes it possible to put the large number of volunteers to work.

Daniel, the young adult librarian, makes supervising these kids look easy. Some of his strategies for working with the teens are best practices that other libraries could try. He believes that the volunteer experience should simulate a paid job as much as possible. Teens should be interviewed as if they were applying for a paid position. They should be formally oriented and trained for the tasks they will be doing. Job descriptions are helpful for both the teens and the adult staff they will be working with. Good work should be acknowledged, and inadequate work corrected. Name tags or other indicators of their formal role are important. The teens seemed to understand the special boundaries of their relationship with Daniel. One said, "I talk a lot with Daniel. He's like my boss, but not really." Another said, "Daniel is kind of like a caretaker for us teens."

Both Daniel and the teens agreed that their volunteer work was meaningful, not just busywork. This was also true of the more than twenty teen volunteers throughout California that I interviewed. One said, "Lunch is so important. It's the only place some of these kids can get it. People come regularly and express their gratitude from their heart." Other quotes from the teen volunteers: "I have always come to this library. Now I can give back." "I can help show kids a better path." "The library is connected to the community."

Another aspect of their jobs that the teens appreciated was interacting with the public. Many volunteers I interviewed said that having to speak with strangers helped them overcome shyness and develop confidence. One said, "I used to be more quiet. Now I'm perky and outgoing. I enjoy being around people at the library." Another said, "I have gotten better at helping people who don't speak English." And still another said, "I've grown as a person. I'm homeschooled, so this helps me be more outgoing."

The Vista Branch is a big, busy library with enough staff to allow Daniel to spend time interviewing, training, and supervising his dozens of teen volunteers. He knows he can delegate some of the supervisory responsibility to other staff who are happy to have the help of well-trained, motivated teens, whether it's shelving books, assisting with children's programs, or checking books out at the circulation desk. The positive outcomes include goodwill from the community, improved capacity to implement special programs like Lunch @ the Library, and a myriad of benefits for the teens who volunteer—personal, marketable, and social skills being the things that the young people mention most often.

Leadership Development

When teens are allowed to work at higher levels of the youth participation ladder, they often decide to put their efforts toward empowering other teens and contributing to their leadership development. In 2007, the young adult services staff at the Cleveland Public Library organized Teen Empowerment: A Motivational Summit (T.E.A.M.S.), a weekend event that gave teens the opportunity to learn more about the services and opportunities available to them in the city. Input from teens was solicited in advance to learn what topics most interested them. The resulting sessions included Chill Out (stress management), Date Rape Awareness, DIVA (leadership for girls), Boys 2 Men (leadership for boys), Managing Your Money, and Get Involved! (volunteerism). This level-5 event reached 262 teens, many of whom requested that the event be held again the following year. It also connected the library with many city and nonprofit agencies eager to promote their services to the city's youth (Alessio 2008).

The Free Library of Philadelphia has had a long-standing commitment to youth development as a part of LEAP (Literacy Enrichment Afterschool Program), an afterschool program implemented at every branch library. Teen leadership assistants (TLAs) are hired to work eight to ten hours a week to provide neighborhood children and other teens with educational and cultural enrichment. The TLAs are also paid to attend Saturday-morning trainings at the main library. These trainings can be job-related, giving teens ideas for programs or tips on customer service. Other topics have included personal safety, college admission strategies, and personal finance.

Additionally, each teen is expected to serve on a committee to plan the annual teen leadership summit. The TLAs like to say that the summit is an event planned *by* teens *for* teens. Typically, about three hundred teens from high schools all over the city attend on a school day in May. There are concurrent workshops on a wide range of topics, such as college financial aid, sexual responsibility, and manga. An inspirational speaker addresses the teens at the end of the day. Community organizations set up tables to distribute information about their services. Some lucky teens walk away with door prizes such as laptop computers, cameras, and gift certificates. The TLAs who have planned the theme, invited community organizations to attend, decided on workshop topics, and invited the guest speaker are always proud of what they have accomplished.

Demonstrating that TLAs are achieving positive youth development outcomes has been part of the Free Library's winning formula for securing grants and regular city funding for LEAP. This is an interesting example of one library's commitment to engaging its young people in meaningful work on behalf of the community. Everyone wins: the library; the children who participate in LEAP, many of whom are from low-income families; and the TLAs, who gain leadership skills as well as a small paycheck (Walter 2009).

In *Teens and Libraries: Getting It Right*, my coauthor Elaine Meyers and I (Walter and Meyers 2003, 123–26) included a Youth Participation Worksheet as a tool for library staff to think about ways to involve teens meaningfully. This worksheet (123) can be applied to any library activity in which teens might participate. It asks the librarian to:

1. List the steps necessary for the task to be completed.
2. Designate which of the steps would be appropriate for teen participation. Check this recommendation with teens.
3. Define the outcomes for teens who participate.
4. List the supports needed for teens.

5. List the opportunities for teens.
6. Design an evaluation that assesses the achievement
   of the desired youth outcomes.

Public libraries can be vital laboratories for teens to develop the skills needed to become active participants in the civic life of their community. This can be done by engaging them as significant advisors in the programs that affect them, by providing meaningful volunteer activities, or by infusing job opportunities with the principles of youth development. If we genuinely invite teens to speak and then listen to them with open ears, we can learn to work with them in ways that ultimately benefit the communities in which we live and work together.

What about the Children?

This chapter has focused on ways that public libraries can promote meaningful civic engagement in teens. What about their younger brothers and sisters? The principles of positive youth development are by now well institutionalized in best practices for young adult library services. These principles lead logically to more youth participation. Are there any similar principles that would lead us to provide opportunities for children to participate actively in the planning and implementation of library services?

In *Twenty-First-Century Kids, Twenty-First-Century Librarians* (Walter 2010), I posited five different models of childhood on which public libraries could base their services to children: the child as reader, the child of the information age, the child in the community, the global child, and the empowered child. All of these have implications for involving children as more active participants in our libraries; but it is the last model—the empowered child—that offers the most powerful rationale. It is based on some of the more recent research and thinking about children's rights. The scholar Barbara Woodhouse (2004, 235–39) posits two categories of rights for children: needs-based rights and dignity-based rights. Needs-based rights acknowledge the dependent nature of childhood and propose rights to nurturance, education, and medical care, for example. Dignity-based rights reflect the developing capacity of children to participate in decisions affecting their own lives. Woodhouse identifies five principles of human rights that can be applied to children (2004, 235–39):

- The equality principle: the right to equal opportunity
- The individualism principles: the right to be treated as a
  person, not an object

- The empowerment principle: the right to a voice and, sometimes, a choice
- The protection principle: the right of the weak to be protected from the strong
- The privacy principle: the right to protection of intimate relationships

I have found this framework to be very useful in resolving much of the tension around the issue of children's rights. It recognizes the child's right to protection as well as the child's right to autonomy. It also offers a rationale for giving children as much of a voice in our library operations as we offer to teens.

It also suggests making some changes in our usual priorities for children's library services. What would happen if we established children's advisory boards? What if we instituted Civic Labs along with our popular maker spaces? What if we involved school-age children in drafting a children's library bill of rights?

There are far fewer examples of exemplary practices that empower children in activities that foster their agency or their civic engagement. However, here are two to consider:

1. At the East Los Angeles Library, children's librarian Sil Ruiz was working with families in a community that is 90 percent Latinx, many of which do not speak English in their homes. During a recent election, she decided to help kids understand the process. It started with a "register to vote" campaign in which children signed up for a pretend presidential election. The older kids nominated a raccoon to be their candidate; the younger kids were supporting a dog. The children decorated a voting booth and talked about the issues. They developed written statements of support for their candidates, held a public forum, and then voted. Proud parents came to hear and support their children as they made their public-speaking debuts.

   This program was so successful in generating information and interest in the voting process that the library system has gone on to develop a civic engagement "program in a box" that will be available to all branches. It is designed to create awareness of voting rights and the Nineteenth Amendment in children, teens, and their families. Among the program ideas are "Run for Pretend President," in which children try to convince their peers that they are the best candidates for the job. Other activities include holding debates on issues like raising the age for getting a driver's license or making vaping illegal for minors, and using a mock election between cats and dogs to explain how the Electoral College works.

2. Meanwhile, in Alameda, a community in California's East Bay, two tween girls started "The Butterfly Effect: Migration Is Beautiful." Kaia and Lillian had been upset when they heard an NPR broadcast about the plight of migrant children being held at the border. Monarch butterflies are often used as a symbol for migration, and the girls started making origami butterflies to raise awareness and support for those detained children. Their goal was to make fifteen thousand, representing the estimated number of children being held at the time. There are now children making butterflies in many parts of the United States, and at least thirty-three thousand have now been assembled. The girls plan to take fifteen thousand to Washington and display them in the Capitol Rotunda. Another fifteen thousand are going to the Office of Refugee Resettlement, where the girls hope the butterflies will be distributed to the detention centers so the migrant children can see them (Serrano 2019).

The story of the Butterfly Effect initiative could just be a story about child activists putting compassion and a global conscience into practice. However, there is a public-library angle to the story. One of the community butterfly-making sessions was held at the Dimond Branch of the Oakland Public Library. The library website invited children to join the butterfly-making movement. It described the Butterfly Effect as a Bay Area youth–led art project whose goal is to create a visual representation of the immigrant children in the detention centers (Oakland Public Library, n.d.).

The keys to engaging children and teens in civic activism at the library are providing both opportunity and support. Public libraries seem to have accepted their responsibility to provide opportunities for teens to engage through advisory boards or councils and volunteer work. There is also increasing awareness of the kinds of support needed to turn those opportunities into meaningful experiences. There is much less recognition of the role that libraries can play in launching children on a path to civic activism. Young role models like Kiyoko (who turned her seventh birthday party into a White House protest) and Kaia and Lillian (who launched the Butterfly Effect initiative) can point us to a more socially conscious form of programming than our customary focus on books and technology. Perhaps teens who have grown into leadership roles as civic activists could help provide age-appropriate support for children who are just finding their voices.

CHAPTER 4

Resources for Civic Literacy

This compilation of recommended print sources is intended to introduce the many good books on topics related to civic literacy and engagement. It is not a comprehensive list. Rather, it is meant to be a place to start.

The first section lists books to share with adults. The remaining books listed here are for children as young as three or four and as old as fourteen or fifteen and can be shared with anyone. I have not included resources specifically for high school students because these teens would be more likely to find the information and inspiration they need in adult titles.

Adult Resources

The Hat-Shaking Dance and Other Ashanti Tales from the Gold Coast. Harold Courlander with Albert Kofi Prempeh. Illustrated by Enrico Arno. New York: Harcourt, 1957.

Storytellers will find some of the best versions of the Ashanti trickster tales in this collection. These are still some of the best representations of the power of the weak to trick and outwit the strong. Much civic activism has been based on this kind of resistance to authority; sharing these stories communicates that message in a nearly subliminal way. Also appropriate for children who love African folktales.

"Libraries Transforming Communities." American Library Association and the Harwood Institute for Public Innovation. Chicago: American Library Association, n.d.

This initiative, a partnership between ALA and the Harwood Institute, aims to strengthen the public library's role as a community leader and change-agent. You can find many practical resources to enable you to implement this initiative on the ALA website, www.ala.org. The "Community Conversation Workbook" is particularly useful.

Library Youth Outreach: 26 Ways to Connect with Children, Young Adults and Their Families. Kerol Harrod and Carol Smallwood, editors. Jefferson, NC: McFarland, 2014.

The contributors to this volume describe many practical, tested strategies for outreach to young people and their families. The ones most relevant to civic literacy and youth engagement are in the chapters on youth focus groups, overnight at the library (which suggests using teen volunteers), and the final chapter on using teen volunteers with children's programming.

Media Literacy and the Emerging Citizen: Youth, Engagement and Participation in Digital Culture. Paul Mihailidis. New York: Peter Lang, 2014.

This is a useful introduction to the connections between digital media, teens, and civic engagement. The author makes a powerful point about the impact of digital media on the political development of teens. While many of his suggestions for facilitating media literacy are best suited to the classroom, others could be incorporated into public library YA services.

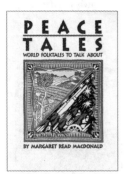

Peace Tales: World Folktales to Talk About. Margaret Read MacDonald. Hamden, CT: Linnet Books, 1992.

This collection of folktales treats the topics of war and peace in a variety of ways. There are Zen tales, such as "Temper" and "Nansen Cuts the Cat in Half." There are fables from Chinese and Indian sources as well as Aesop. Traditional stories from many different parts of the world contain moral lessons wrapped in an entertaining plot. The final story, "Holding Up the Sky," originally told in China, is so short that any librarian could learn it and tell it as a closing to almost any presentation for children or adults. It is a reminder that each of us must do what we can to avert disaster or injustice; together we can do it.

Powered by Girl: A Field Guide for Supporting Youth Activists. Lyn Mikel Brown. Boston: Beacon Press, 2016.

The author presents a strong rationale and good advice for supporting young women in intergenerational collaborations. This is a strong feminist voice, urging girls not to just "lean in" but to believe in their own ideas, raise their own voices, and create their own movements for change. The author makes a case for helping girls find the strong female role models that are often missing from their history textbooks and classroom learning. That is something librarians can do.

Shake-It-Up Tales: Stories to Sing, Dance, Drum, and Act Out. Margaret Read MacDonald. Atlanta: August House, 2000.

This is a treasure house of stories that encourage audience participation. They are great fun to tell, but many also contain subtle messages about cooperation, kindness, empathy, and resistance to injustice. Use these to enliven a presentation, start a conversation, and spread civic literacy.

Social Justice and Activism in Libraries: Essays on Diversity and Change. Su Epstein, Carol Smallwood, and Vera Gubnitskaia, editors. Jefferson, NC: Macfarland, 2019.

The essays in this volume cover many strategies for addressing social justice in different kinds of libraries—those in educational institutions, archives, and prisons as well as public libraries. Taken as a whole, they give inspiration and provide an ideological rationale as well as practical examples for other activist librarians.

Teen-Centered Library Service: Putting Youth Participation into Practice. Diane P. Tuccillo. Santa Barbara, CA: Libraries Unlimited, 2010.

This practical guide provides a rationale for meaningful youth participation in public libraries and offers a detailed menu of strategies for recruiting teen participants, training them, and creating meaningful opportunities for getting involved. These range from sponsoring traditional teen advisory boards and other volunteer activities to civic engagement and community outreach to including teens in evaluation efforts and service on adult library boards.

Using Nonfiction for Civic Engagement in Classrooms: Critical Approaches. Vivian Yankia-Agbaw, Ruth McKoy Lowery, and Paul H. Ricks. Lanham, MD: Rowman & Littlefield, 2018.

While the intended readership for this book is classroom teachers, librarians working with children and teens will find much relevant content here. Chapter 2, for example, focuses on young civil rights activists; chapter 5 explores ways that reading nonfiction titles can help sixth graders understand the Japanese internment camps of World War II. The book is full of recommended titles—mostly for middle school students—and suggestions for using these books to foster critical literacy. There are strategies here that a public librarian could use with a book discussion group or teen advisory board. This is also a good book for teachers who might be looking for new titles to share with their students.

Activism and Children

A Is for Activist. Innosanto Nagara. New York: Triangle Square, 2013.
GRADES PRE-K-3.

Written and illustrated for the author's young son, this is a book best shared with young children by adults or caregivers who share these leftist political values. This could be a good conversation starter about political and social issues that seem otherwise too abstract for the very youngest people in our communities.

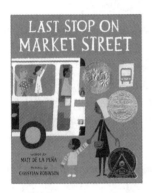

Last Stop on Market Street. Matt de la Peña. Illustrated by Christian Robinson. New York: G. P. Putnam's Sons, 2015.
GRADES PRE-K-2.

A small boy reluctantly accompanies his grandmother on a long bus ride across the city to the soup kitchen where they volunteer to help feed the hungry. When they arrive, a rainbow arches above the building, and C. J. sees familiar faces waiting for them. "I'm glad we came," he says. His grandmother pats him on the head and tells him, "Me too, C. J. Now come on." This brief picture book was awarded the Newbery Medal for its simple eloquence. Adults will welcome its message that even the youngest child can feel empathy and be empowered to help others.

Never Too Young: 50 Unstoppable Kids Who Made a Difference. Aileen Weintraub. Illustrated by Laura Horton. New York: Sterling Children's Books, 2018.
GRADES 3-5.

This book gives one-page profiles of fifty people who accomplished big things when they were still young. Some are activists—such as Thandiwe Chama, who organized children for education rights in her native Zambia, and Yash Gupta, who started a nonprofit organization to provide eyeglasses to students around the world. Some are famous—like Malala Yousafzai and Nadia Comanici. There are philanthropists, inventors, musicians, athletes, and artists—somebody to inspire almost any child.

Political Activism: How You Can Make a Difference. Heather E. Schwartz. New York: Capstone Press, 2009. GRADES 3–6.

This is a brief, accessible guide to activism for school-age children. There are profiles of young people who have engaged effectively with the political system as well as specific suggestions for doing research, setting goals, and getting the attention of people in power.

Say Something. Peter H. Reynolds. New York: Scholastic/Orchard, 2019. GRADES K–2.

This slight picture book encourages young children to speak up and say something when they see something wrong, or when they have a good new idea or are inspired in any way. This book doesn't offer a lot of substance, but it could start a useful conversation or empower some children to think of themselves as agents for change.

What Can a Citizen Do? Dave Eggers. Illustrated by Shawn Harris. San Francisco: Chronicle Books, 2018. GRADES K–3.

A diverse group of children answer that question by collaborating on a project to build a build a tower on an island. The message is sometimes a little obscure: "A citizen can be a bear." Overall, however, this is a celebration of the positive energy that our youngest children can bring to creating a better society by being active citizens.

You Are Mighty: A Guide to Changing the World. Caroline Paul. Illustrated by Lauren Tamaki. New York: Bloomsbury, 2018. GRADES 3–6.

While most of the guides to activism for young people are aimed at teens, this one is appropriate for much younger children. The author doesn't tell her readers what they should stand for (or against). Instead she provides a lot of information about what even young children can do in their quest for justice. Some of the strategies she suggests include making a protest sign, writing letters, boycotting, using social media, marching, or organizing a sit-in. She gives many examples of kids who have actually done these things. Ten-year-old Mia Hansen gathered more than 150,000 signatures on a petition to Jamba Juice to stop using Styrofoam cups—and got them to do it. Ten-year-old Samantha Smith wrote to Yuri Andropov, the new president of the Soviet Union, in 1982. She asked him what he was going to do to prevent a war between her country and his. He wrote back, expressing his desire for peace. Samantha was invited to visit the Soviet Union, and eleven-year-old Katya Lycheva visited America. Other, less dramatic examples include children who became vegan when they learned how chicken nuggets are made or those who stopped using plastic straws when they heard what plastic does to our oceans. Young activists can find a lot of inspiration here, along with practical tips for changing the world.

Activism and Teens

Activism: The Ultimate Teen Guide. Kathlyn Gay. Lanham, MD: Rowman & Littlefield, 2016.
GRADES 7 AND UP.

The author begins this book with an interesting distinction between being a volunteer and being an activist. She writes that volunteers become activists when they come across a problem that requires more than one person at a time to fix it. Subsequent chapters deal with youth rights, advocacy for teen health, animal advocacy, environmental concerns, religious activism, gun control, peace efforts, immigration reform, and more. These overviews are informative, but readers will need to look to other resources for specific strategies to take action themselves.

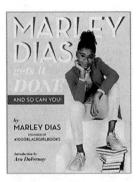

Marley Dias Gets It Done and So Can You! Marley Dias with Siobhán McGowan. New York: Scholastic, 2018.
GRADES 6 AND UP.

When Marley was in sixth grade, she loved to read but was dismayed that there weren't many books about black girls like her. She decided to do something about it. She started the #1000blackgirlbooks initiative to identify, collect, and distribute one thousand books that feature black girls as the main characters. Her social media skills and charismatic personality attracted supporters like Hillary Clinton, Ellen DeGeneres, Michelle Obama, and Ava DuVernay, who wrote an introduction to this book. Teens—especially black girls like Marley—will find both inspiration and practical advice about becoming social activists themselves. The breezy, conversational writing style and highly graphic format make this an attractive and appealing read for the intended audience.

Online Activism: Social Change through Social Media. Amanda Vink. New York: Lucent, 2019.
GRADES 9 AND UP.

The introduction begins with an account of the Arab Spring in 2011, in which mass protests in Egypt—launched in large part on social media such as Facebook— resulted in the resignation of President Hosni Mubarak. Subsequent chapters give a history of online activism, with a special focus on grassroots activism. Attention is given to both hacktivism (the use of computer hacking for the purpose of activism, usually done by those in the digital world to address perceived injustices) and slacktivism (defined here as endorsing a cause online without taking any direct and personal action). A final chapter gives advice for being an ethical, responsible, and effective online activist.

Teen Power Politics: Make Yourself Heard. Sara Jane Boyers. Brookfield, CT: Millbrook, 2000.
GRADES 7 AND UP.

This is an older title than some of the other guides to activism listed here, but its emphasis on electoral politics makes it unique and still timely. The author makes a strong case for those eighteen and older to exercise their right to vote and for younger teens to begin paying more attention to politics. She gives many examples of political issues that affect teens—from cutbacks at the local public swimming pool to a shortage of textbooks in a required high school class to a polluted stream at a favorite camping spot. There are inspiring profiles of teens who made an impact on the political system. Readers will also find resources with URLs, addresses, and phone numbers for young people who want to learn more.

Activism—Inspiration and Role Models

Anansi the Spider: A Tale from the Ashanti. Gerald McDermott. New York: Holt, 1972.
GRADES PRE-K–3.

Anansi is the quintessential folk trickster, and this is one of the best picture books about him. In this story, he is helped by his six sons, and we learn why the moon is up in the sky. Another good story with a subtle subversive message, McDermott's *Raven: A Trickster Tale from the Pacific Northwest* (New York: Harcourt Brace Jovanovich, 1993) is also worth sharing.

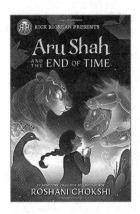

Aru Shah and the End of Time. Roshani Choksi. New York: Disney Hyperion, 2018.
GRADES 5–9.

Aru is forbidden to even touch the Lamp of Barata, an artifact in the museum where her mother works. However, not only does she touch it, but she lights it and releases the Sleeper, an ancient demon who threatens to awaken the god of destruction. It is up to Aru to avert this disaster, and that means a voyage through the Kingdom of Death. This is the first in a series of Pandava novels, all steeped in Hindu mythology.

Biddy Mason Speaks Up. Arisa White and Laura Atkins. Illustrated by Laura Freeman. Berkeley, CA: Heyday, 2019.
GRADES 3–6.

Born a slave in Georgia, where she learns the skills of midwifery and herbal healing, Biddy Mason is brought to Utah and then to California by people who think of her as their property. Slavery is illegal in Los Angeles, but Robert Smith continues to hold Mason and her children captive. During those four years, she manages to develop relationships with free black people living there; and when Smith threatens to take Biddy Mason and her children with him to Texas—a slave state—she is finally able to resist. Eventually there is a trial, and the judge legally declares Biddy Mason and her children free in January of 1856. She goes on to become a landowner and prominent member of the black community. This book intersperses historical background from primary source material with this account of her life. Biddy Mason's story is remarkable for her resilience and her ability to make connections to other people.

Borreguita and the Coyote: A Tale from Ayutla, Mexico. Verna Aardema. Illustrated by Petra Mathers. New York: Knopf, 1991.

How will the little lamb escape the hungry coyote? By using her wits, of course. This is an inspiring story for small children who often feel powerless. Use it in a storytime with theme of empowerment and resistance.

Bruh Rabbit and the Tar Baby Girl. Virginia Hamilton. Illustrations by James E. Ransome. New York: Blue Sky Press, 2000.
GRADES K–3.

Here is a retelling of the traditional African American story in Hamilton's beautifully paced Gullah dialect. Share this at a family storytime to remind everyone that you can get the better of the wolf if you just use your wits.

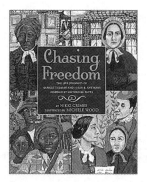

Chasing Freedom: The Life Journeys of Harriet Tubman and Susan B. Anthony, Inspired by Historical Facts. Nikki Grimes. Illustrated by Michele Wood. New York: Orchard Books, 2015. GRADES 2–5.

Nikki Grimes imagines an afternoon of conversation between Harriet Tubman and Susan B. Anthony in 1904, at the 28th Annual Convention of the New York State Suffrage Association. Anthony reminisces about her childhood in a family that believed in equal rights for women, her early meeting with Frederick Douglas, and her years working for the temperance movement. Tubman recalls her escape from slavery and her decision to go back South to rescue members of her family still in bondage. They speak of the many challenges they faced as they continued to work on behalf of votes for women and an end to slavery in the United States. This is a compelling introduction to two remarkable women today's children deserve to know.

Conejito: A Folktale from Panama. Margaret Read MacDonald. Illustrated by Geraldo Valerio. Atlanta: August House, 2006.

On his way to visit his Tia Monica, Conejito succeeds in tricking the fox, the tiger, and the lion, who all want to eat him for lunch. After Tia Monica stuffs him with good things to eat, he is even more tempting to those predators. Fortunately, Tia Monica has another trick up her sleeve, and Conejito is able to get home safely. The story is full of possibilities for getting your listeners up to sing and dance, and they will absorb the moral of the story without feeling preached at. You can also find this story in MacDonald's *Shake-It-Up Tales*, listed under "Adult Resources."

Dragon Pearl. Yoo Ha Lee. New York: Disney Hyperion, 2019. GRADES 5–9.

Min is descended from a long line of fox spirits, but her mother insists that she not use any of her shape-shifting magical powers. So she looks and acts like any ordinary thirteen-year-old girl living in a Korea of the future. When her brother, a member of the Space Forces, is accused of deserting his post, Min decides to clear his name. She will encounter dragons, ghosts, and pirates in a world drawn from Korean folklore in this adventure.

Groundbreaking Guys: 40 Men Who Became Great by Doing Good. Stephanie True Peters. Illustrated by Shamel Washington. New York: Little, Brown, 2019. GRADES 3–5.

Not all the men profiled here would be considered civic activists, but they have all contributed to the good of the world, whether or not this was their primary career. Some are well-known celebrities such as Yo-Yo Ma, Kendrick Lamar, George Clooney, and Kareen Abdul-Jabbar. Others are less familiar, such as Dalip Singh Saund and Carlos Slim Helu. Source notes provide additional documentation. This is an attractive book, with full-color illustrations for each one-page bio, that could be inspirational to those searching for male role models.

Jack Outwits the Giants. Paul Brett Johnson. New York: McElderry, 2002. GRADES K–3.

The giants want to eat Jack, but he's too clever for them. This lively Appalachian tale reinforces the notion that the little guy can beat the big guys if he's smart enough. This is a good choice for a family storytime. Tell it with a mountain twang if you can pull it off.

Just a Minute: A Trickster and Counting Book. Yuyi Morales. San Francisco: Chronicle Books, 2003. GRADES K–3.

When death in the form of Señor Calavera comes for Grandma Beetle, she changes his mind by counting to ten while she calmly goes about preparing for her birthday celebration. The story and illustrations are filled with Mexican and Mexican American themes and motifs; some adults will recognize the logo used by Cesar Chavez and the United Farmworkers in one of the illustrations. This story is funny as well as empowering.

Mandela: The Hero Who Led His Nation to Freedom. Ann Kramer. New York: National Geographic, 2005. GRADES 4–7.

Today's children may not know about the evils of apartheid in South Africa or about Nelson Mandela's role in ridding his country of it. This book is a good corrective to that, presenting Mandela's activist life in the context of the political situation in his country. See also the children's version of his adult autobiography: *Nelson Mandela: Long Walk to Freedom*, abridged by Chris VanWyk (listed on following page).

Nelson Mandela: Long Walk to Freedom. Nelson Mandela. Abridged by Chris VanWyk. Illustrated by Paddy Bouma. New York: Roaring Brook Press, 2010. GRADES 2–5.

The basic facts about the life and work of this Nobel Peace Prize medalist are here: his childhood, education, and growing awareness that he must act to end apartheid, even if it means imprisonment. This is a man that children should know about. See also *Mandela: The Hero Who Led His Nation to Freedom* by Ann Kramer (listed on preveious page) for older children.

Shaking Things Up: 14 Young Women Who Changed the World. Susan Hood. New York: Harper, 2018. GRADES K–3.

These short profiles in poetry with illustrations by thirteen different women artists range from six-year-old Ruby Bridges and seventeen-year-old Malala Yousafzai (discussed elsewhere in this book) to journalist Nellie Bly, World War II secret agents Jacqueline and Eileen Nearne, architect Maya Lin, and antihunger activist Frances Moore Lappé. Most of the women featured here were in their twenties when they did great things to change the world. Hopefully, young readers—both boys and girls—will find inspiration here.

The Storm Runner. J. C. Cervantes. New York: Disney Hyperion, 2018. GRADES 5–9.

When Zane Obispo unwittingly releases Ah-Puch, a Mayan god of great destructive power, he learns that he is actually the person prophesied to kill Ah-Puch himself. Not only that, but Zane is a demigod, the son of the Mayan god Hurakan. What follows this revelation is an adventure into the dark world of Mayan mythology. These are not the capricious Roman and Greek gods that we might be more familiar with; but these gods are also capable of great violence when their power is threatened.

The Tale of Rabbit and Coyote. Tony Johnston. Illustrated by Tomie dePaola. New York: Putnam, 1994. GRADES K–3.

In this picture-book trickster tale from Oaxaca, Mexico, Rabbit gets the best of Coyote. This story brings together many familiar threads, such as the American Brer Rabbit tale and the "rabbit in the moon." It is as colorful and spicy as the chile patch where Rabbit is stuck at the beginning of the story.

Tristan Strong Punches a Hole in the Sky. Kwame Mbalia. New York: Disney Hyperion, 2019.
GRADES 5–9.

Tristan Strong does not feel strong. He had failed to save his best friend when they were in a bus accident. Now he has been sent to his grandparents' farm in Alabama to recover from the accident. His first night there he manages to tear a hole in the sky and ends up working with Brer Rabbit and John Henry to coax Anansi to mend the rip. Seventh grader Tristan's adventures are imbued with American and Ashanti folklore.

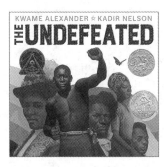

The Undefeated. Kwame Alexander. Illustrated by Kadir Nelson. Boston: Houghton Mifflin/ Versify, 2019.
GRADES 2–5.

This illustrated poem is a powerful tribute to the strength and resilience of African Americans who persevered in spite of overwhelming obstacles. These are not all activists as we understand the term (although John Lewis and Dr. Martin Luther King Jr. are pictured and mentioned by name). The inclusion of artists, writers, musicians, and athletes expands the message of empowerment and makes it very accessible to the black children for whom this book is primarily intended.

We Are All in the Dumps with Jack and Guy: Two Nursery Rhymes with Pictures. Maurice Sendak. New York: HarperCollins, 1993.
ALL AGES.

Sendak's illustrations transform two little-known nursery rhymes into scathing social commentary about homelessness and hunger. Take your time with this book and really look at the pictures. Who will be the first to find the reference to Trump and his tower in New York?

We Rise, We Resist, We Raise Our Voices. Wade Hudson and Cheryl Willis Hudson. New York: Crown Books for Young Readers, 2018.
ALL AGES.

This anthology of poems, essays, letters, and pictures is a resource begging to be shared with children who may feel discouraged by the current state of our country and the failure of adult leadership to fix things. It is filled with words and images that encourage children to become activists for change themselves. Most of the contributors are African American, and there are many references to the civil rights movement; but Latinx, Asian, and American Indian authors and artists are represented here as well.

Activism—War and Peace

See also "Nonviolent Protest."

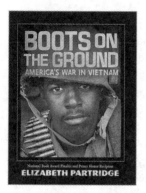

Boots on the Ground: America's War in Vietnam. Elizabeth Partridge. New York: Viking, 2018. GRADES 5–8.

Perspectives on the Vietnam War are presented through profiles of individuals involved on many levels and in many different ways. There are three American presidents who governed from the beginning to the end of the war: John F. Kennedy, Lyndon B. Johnson, and Richard Nixon. There are individual soldiers and an army nurse. Hoa Thi Nguyen, a refugee from Vietnam, is represented. Two antiwar activists have their say: Dr. Martin Luther King Jr. and protest singer Country Joe McDonald. Maya Lin, the designer of the Vietnam Veterans Memorial in Washington, DC, encountered some hostility from people who were outraged that an Asian woman would be given this responsibility. She responded, "That's irrelevant. This is America."

The Champ: The Story of Muhammad Ali. Tonya Bolden. Illustrated by R. Gregory Christie. New York: Knopf, 2004. GRADES 3–5.

Most children are aware of Muhammad Ali only as a boxing champion. This picture-book biography focuses on his refusal to be drafted in 1967 because of his religious beliefs and opposition to the war in Vietnam. He is threatened with a prison sentence, and his passport is revoked. After three years of public speaking about his opposition to the war and the struggles of African Americans, the US Supreme Court finally rules that he cannot be jailed for his resistance to the draft on religious grounds. See also Charles R. Smith's *Twelve Rounds to Glory* (listed later in this section) for older children.

The Fragile Flag. Jane Langton. New York: Harper, 1984; HarperTrophy, 1989. GRADES 4–6.

Georgie decides to walk to Washington, DC, to hand-deliver her letter to the president, telling him "what the flag of our country means to me." Her solitary walk turns into a children's crusade as thousands of children join her to protest the president's "Peace Missile."

Fred Korematsu Speaks Up. Laura Atkins and Stan Yogi. Illustrated by Yutaka Houlette. Berkeley, CA: Heyday, 2017.

AGES 4–8.

As a teenager, Fred Korematsu does not turn himself in when the US government ordered all Japanese Americans on the West Coast to be evacuated into internment camps. He is arrested and sent to the camps anyway. Ernest Besig, an ACLU lawyer, argues Fred's case against the internment all the way to the Supreme Court but is not successful. After the war, Korematsu marries and raises his children, trying to put that unhappy past behind him. In the 1980s, researchers find documents in the National Archives that prove the government attorneys lied when they claimed to have evidence that Japanese Americans on the West Cost were signaling to Japanese submarines and ships; there was no military necessity for the Japanese to be locked away for the duration of the war. Korematsu agrees to be part of the lawsuit that eventually overturned his conviction and paved the way for an official apology from the federal government and the granting of reparations to those who were interned. A brief afterword gives suggestions to young people who want to speak up for justice.

Letters from Wolfie. Patti Sherlock. New York: Viking, 2004.

GRADES 6–9.

Thirteen-year-old Mark wants to do his part for the war effort now that his older brother Danny has volunteered to fight in Vietnam. He donates his German shepherd, Wolfie, to be trained as a scout dog. He is shaken when Wolfie's trainer writes that the dog isn't as aggressive as it should be. Mark tries to get Wolfie returned to him, but the dog is now "army equipment." Then he starts dating a girl whose brother has gone to Canada to avoid the war, and Danny returns with one leg amputated at the knee and a new conviction that the war was all wrong. Wolfie doesn't return at all, dying on a scouting expedition in Vietnam. This book may help young readers of today understand the conflicts that can arise in a family over differing opinions and perspectives and also acquire a context for understanding the Vietnam War years.

Nim and the War Effort. Milly Lee. Illustrated by Yangsook Choi. New York: Farrar, Straus and Giroux, 1997.
GRADES 2–4.

It is World War II, in San Francisco's Chinatown. Nim is determined to collect the most newspapers in her school's paper drive to help the war effort. Her efforts take her beyond the boundaries of her neighborhood and almost get her in trouble with her strict grandfather. In the end, however, Nim is able to make her grandfather proud as well as demonstrate her patriotism as a true American.

Number the Stars. Lois Lowry. Boston: Houghton Mifflin, 1989.
GRADES 4–6.

Activism in wartime has often taken the form of resistance to authority. During World War II, there were many examples of civilians risking their own lives to rescue Jews from the horrors of the Holocaust. This Newbery Medal winner tells how a young Danish girl bravely does her part to save her Jewish friend Ellen from the Nazis.

Paths to Peace: People Who Changed the World. Jane Breskin Zallben. New York: Dutton, 2006.
GRADES 4–8.

Sixteen peacemakers are given one-page profiles in this handsome book. Zallben points out in her introduction that many of them owe their commitment to working for a more peaceful world to childhood influences. Many of the people here— Anwar Sadat, Ralph Bunche, and Elie Wiesel, for example—are well known for their activism, even receiving the Nobel Peace Prize. Others, such as Princess Diana and Albert Einstein, are probably better known for other contributions to the world. Together, they all form an inspiring cadre of role models for today's young people.

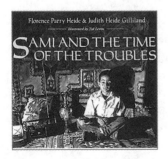

Sami and the Time of the Troubles. Florence Parry Heide and Judith Heide Gilliland. Illustrated by Ted Lewin. New York: Clarion, 1992.
GRADES 2–4.

Sami is a ten-year-old Lebanese boy who lives in a country that has been at war for his entire life. His father was killed by a bomb, and now he and his mother and little sister live with his uncle and his grandfather. Most days the family stays in the basement in order to be safe from the guns and fighting. His grandfather sometimes tells him about a day when children appeared on the streets with banners, flags, and signs that said, "Stop the fighting." Sami tells his grandfather that it may be time for another day when the children march for peace, and his grandfather answers that, this time, maybe the ones who fight will listen.

Shooting the Moon. Frances O'Roark Dowell. New York: Atheneum, 2008. GRADES 5–7.

Twelve-year-old Jamie is thrilled when her brother goes to Vietnam to fight. She anticipates getting letters filled with descriptions of exciting combat and heroism. Instead she gets a roll of film that, when developed, reveals a dark side to the US Army's role there and a threat to her brother's safety. What can a little sister do?

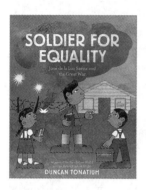

Soldier for Equality: José de la Luz Sáenz and the Great War. Duncan Tonatiuh. New York: Abrams, 2019. GRADES 3–5.

This is the true story of José de la Luz Sáenz, who leaves his job teaching in a small town in Texas to fight in World War I. He has experienced prejudice and discrimination against Mexican Americans at home but expects to find more justice and equality in the military. Those expectations are not met; he returns home after the war and joins with two other Mexican American veterans to form the League of United Latin American Citizens in 1929. LULAC, the oldest and largest civil rights organization serving the Latinx community, joined lawsuits to end school segregation of Mexican American children, worked to end the exclusion of Mexican Americans from juries and as registered voters, and continues to fight for immigration rights.

Stop This War! American Protest of the Conflict in Vietnam. Margot Fortunato Galt. Minneapolis: Lerner, 2000. GRADES 6–9.

The author introduces the tradition of pacifism in the first chapter and then goes on to tell how the Vietnam War generated activism among a new generation of antiwar protesters. She writes about the young men who went to Canada to avoid the draft, campus sit-ins, marches, vigils, and moments of violence in what was intended to be a nonviolent movement. The book closes with a brief section on the Vietnam Veterans Memorial designed by Maya Ying Lin as a wall of loss and healing. There is an excellent bibliography of additional resources, all written for adults but accessible to teens who want to know more.

Twelve Rounds to Glory: The Story of Muhammad Ali. Charles R. Smith. Illustrated by Bryan Collier Jr. Somerville, MA: Candlewick, 2007.
GRADES 5 AND UP.

The rhythm of rap combines with watercolor collage illustrations to make an appealing account of the boxing champ and activist's life. Introduce this book to children, especially boys, as a companion to Tonya Bolden's *The Champ* (listed earlier in this section).

Vietnam: A History of the War. Russell Freedman. New York: Holiday House, 2016.
GRADES 5–8.

A well-researched, well-documented account of the events leading up to the Vietnam War, America's involvement, and the aftermath. Includes a good chapter on the antiwar movement's young activists and adult supporters.

We Will Not Be Silent: The White Rose Student Resistance Movement that Defied Adolf Hitler. Russell Freedman. New York: Clarion Books, 2016.
GRADES 5–9.

A heartbreaking but inspirational account of the resistance movement against Hitler's totalitarian regime, mounted by university students based in Munich. Working in deep secrecy, they write and distribute leaflets that urge their fellow Germans to resist the government. The leaders are ultimately arrested and killed by guillotine, leaving a legacy of courage and commitment to truth and justice.

The Yellow Star: The Legend of King Christian X of Denmark. Carmen Agra Deedy. Illustrated by Henri Sorenson. Atlanta: Peachtree, 2000.
GRADES 2–4.

During World War II, the Danes quietly and often effectively resisted German efforts to deport their Jewish citizens. This picture book tells the legend of the Danish king Christian. The story goes that when the Nazis ordered all Danish Jews to wear the six-pointed yellow star, King Christian wore a star on his own uniform when he went out on his daily horse ride.

Bullying

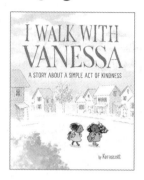

I Walk with Vanessa: A Story about a Simple Act of Kindness. Kerascoët. New York: Schwartz & Wade Books, 2018.

GRADES K–3.

Nobody offers to walk home with the new girl in class, so she sets off by herself. One of the students sees her being bullied and worries about it all night. The next morning that student goes to the new girl's house, and they walk to school together. They are joined by another child, and another and another, until it looks like her whole class is walking her to school. This wordless picture book shows the power and contagion of a simple act of kindness.

Super Manny Stands Up! Kelly DiPucchio. Illustrated by Stephanie Graegin. New York: Atheneum, 2017.

GRADES K–2.

Manny is a little boy raccoon who wears a different color cape every day to give him superpowers as he battles imaginary monsters and evil of all kinds. For school, he wears an invisible cape. In the lunchroom one day, he sees a big bully teasing a little kid. At first Manny is frozen with fear. Then he remembers that he is a superhero with an invisible cape and says, "Stop it." Soon all the other children put on their invisible capes and join him until the bully retreats. This is an age-appropriate message for small children about finding and using their own superpowers for good.

The Civil Rights Movement

See also "Nonviolent Protest."

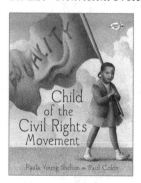

Child of the Civil Rights Movement. Paula Young Shelton. Illustrated by Raúl Colón. New York: Random House, 2010.

GRADES 2–5.

The daughter of civil rights leader and UN Ambassador Andrew Young writes about growing up in a family that revolved around the early civil rights movement. Dr. Martin Luther King Jr. was Uncle Martin and Coretta Scott King was Aunt Coretta to Paula and her sisters. When Paula was four years old, she participated with her family in the historic march from Selma to Montgomery—sometimes marching, often being carried by one of the grownups. In 1965, she watches TV with her family as President Lyndon Johnson signs the Voting Rights Act. "And one day, when Mama and Daddy were too tired to march, too weary to carry us on their shoulders, too exhausted to fight another battle, the baton would pass to us and we would march on—children of the civil rights movement."

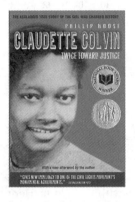

Claudette Colvin: Twice toward Justice. Philip Hoose. New York: Farrar, Straus and Giroux, 2009. GRADES 6–9.

Before there was Rosa Parks, there was Claudette Colvin. In 1955, this high school junior refuses to give up her seat on a Montgomery city bus to a white woman. She is arrested and faces three charges: violating the city's segregation law, disturbing the peace, and assaulting the policeman who threw her off the bus. She is found guilty of all charges and placed on probation in the custody of her parents. She and three other women later challenge the law requiring segregated seating on municipal buses. When they win, in *Browder v. Gayle*, the buses are finally integrated. Hoose writes about Claudette's upbringing in a state ruled by Jim Crow laws and traditions, where her mother once slapped her for letting a white boy touch her hands. (Touching a white person was just one of the things that was forbidden.) Claudette was inspired to resist when ordered to give up her seat on the bus by what she had learned about her constitutional rights in a high school class. This is a story that any teen faced with injustice could relate to.

A Dream of Freedom: The Civil Rights Movement from 1954 to 1968.
Diane McWhorter. New York: Scholastic, 2004.
GRADES 5–8.

The author is a Southern woman raised by a white supremacist father in Birmingham, Alabama. Her well-documented and thorough overview of the civil rights movement is interwoven with her own growing awareness of the injustice done to black people by the segregationist policies in her city and throughout the South. This account includes the events leading up to such pivotal events as the Montgomery bus boycott, the lunch counter sit-ins, Freedom Rides, the March on Washington, Mississippi Freedom Summer, the Selma march, the Watts uprising, and finally, the death of Dr. Martin Luther King Jr. in Memphis in 1968. Sources for further reading lists websites as well as eight books.

Freedom Walkers: The Story of the Montgomery Bus Boycott. Russell
Freedman. New York: Holiday House, 2006.
GRADES 4–6.

Freedman provides important background and context to the yearlong boycott by
black people in Montgomery, Alabama. He also documents the violent backlash
from the white community to this struggle. It is a testament to the leadership of
people like Dr. Martin Luther King Jr. and Ralph Abernathy and to the persistence
and resilience of ordinary people who had finally had enough of oppression and
resisted with such tenacity.

***Freedom's Children: Young Civil Rights Activists
Tell Their Own Stories.*** Ellen Levine. New York:
Putnam, 1993.
GRADES 5–8.

Black children and teens were active and visible participants in the civil rights movement in the South. They
marched, demonstrated, protested, participated in sit-ins,
and were arrested and jailed along with the adults. Here
are the stories, in their own words, of some of those activists who were there for the Montgomery bus boycott, the
Freedom Rides, the lunch counter sit-ins, and other major
events of the 1950s and '60s. Ellen Levine gives background on each event and then
presents the first-person accounts of those young people.

Let the Children March. Monica Clark-Robinson. Illustrated by Frank Morrison.
Boston: Houghton Mifflin Harcourt, 2018.
GRADES 2–4.

In 1963, Dr. Martin Luther King Jr. stood in a black church in Birmingham, Alabama,
and asked the congregation to join him on a march demanding an end to segregation of public places in the city—a march that would involve civil disobedience,
arrests, and jail for participants. When the adults expressed unwillingness to risk
their jobs, the children offered to march in their place. At first the parents said no,
but Dr. King said, "Let the children march." This is the story of two of those children who marched proudly, were arrested, and saw the successful results of their
activism when segregation laws in the city were overturned.

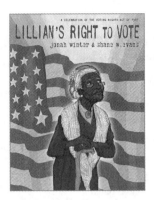

Lillian's Right to Vote: A Celebration of the Voting Rights Act of 1965. Jonah Winter. Illustrated by Shane W. Evans. New York: Schwartz Wade Books, 2015. GRADES 3–5.

As hundred-year-old Lillian walks the long, steep hill to the courthouse to vote for the first time in her life, she remembers the many black people before her who were refused that basic right of citizenship. There were her great-great-great-grandparents who were slaves. Great-Grandpa Edmund was born a slave but acquired the right to vote when the Fifteenth Amendment was passed in 1870. His wife could not vote, however, because women were still denied that right. Grandpa Isaac could not pay the newly enacted poll tax, and Uncle Levi was unable to pass the "test" required of all black would-be voters. In 1920, the Nineteenth Amendment made it possible for Lillian's mother to vote; but an angry mob of white men chased her away when she tried to register, and a cross was burned on her lawn to drive home the point. Lillian remembers the first time she tried to register to vote herself but was unable to write down verbatim the words of a section of the US Constitution, which was purposely mumbled by the registrar. But now it is 1965. Years of protests and marches have finally resulted in the Voting Rights Act—and nothing is going to stop this old woman from voting.

March On! The Day My Brother Martin Changed the World. Christine King Farris. Illustrated by London Ladd. New York: Scholastic, 2008. GRADES 2–4.

This picture-book account of the March on Washington in 1963 presents this event from the perspective of Dr. Martin Luther King Jr. His sister tells how he spends the night before the march by himself in the Willard Hotel, writing and rewriting the speech he would give. The turnout exceeds anyone's expectations, and King's "I Have a Dream" speech does indeed make a change in the political climate for equal rights for blacks in America.

One Crazy Summer. Rita Williams-Garcia. New York: HarperCollins, 2010. GRADES 4–7.

It is 1968. Eleven-year-old Delphine and her two little sisters are sent by their father from their home in Brooklyn to Oakland, California, to spend the summer with their mother Cecile, who had abandoned them when the youngest girl was just a baby. Cecile does not seem happy to see them and doesn't even feed them, serving up Chinese takeout for supper and sending the girls to the center run by the Black

Panthers for breakfast and summer camp. Little by little, Delphine begins to understand the political rhetoric of resistance to racism and injustice that is taught at the center. When Delphine's mother is arrested along with two of the brothers from the Black Panthers, the three sisters respond with righteous militant anger. When they leave to go back to Brooklyn, they finally get what they wanted from their mother all along: a big hug. This book is a tribute to sisters and mothers as well as an intimate glimpse of one of the most important grassroots activist groups in the history of our country.

A Place to Land: Martin Luther King Jr. and the Speech That Inspired a Nation. Barry Wittenstein. Illustrated by Jerry Pinkney. New York: Holiday House, 2019.
GRADES 2–5.

This is a clear, nuanced portrait in words and images of the people (mostly men) and ideas that influenced Dr. Martin Luther King Jr. as he prepared and gave his famous "I Have a Dream" speech at the 1963 March on Washington. It might bring tears to your eyes.

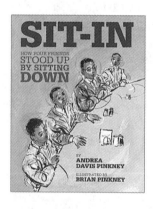

Sit-In: How Four Friends Stood Up by Sitting Down. Andrea Davis Pinkney. Illustrated by Brian Pinkney. New York: Little Brown, 2010.
GRADES 2–4.

A short but informative and evocative account of the Woolworth lunch counter sit-ins that began in Greensboro, North Carolina, and spread to many Southern states where public eating places were segregated. The students who conducted the sit-ins were following Dr. Martin Luther King Jr.'s philosophy of nonviolence. Partially because of these efforts, the Civil Rights Act of 1964 was passed, banning segregation in public places. A useful timeline of major civil rights events is included.

To the Mountaintop: My Journey through the Civil Rights Movement. Charlayne Hunter-Gault. New York: Roaring Brook Press, 2012.
GRADES 5–9.

Young readers may not know of Hunter-Gault, but many of their parents and grandparents will remember her from the *MacNeil/Lehrer NewsHour*. Her memoir starts with the inauguration of Barack Obama as the nation's first black president in 2009 and moves back in time to her days as a young activist in the civil rights movement in the South. She was there for many of the pivotal events of the movement, and that firsthand perspective lends to the immediacy of her accounts. A timeline and selected relevant articles from the *New York Times* add value.

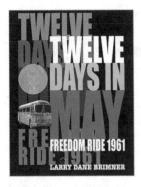

Twelve Days in May: Freedom Ride 1961. Larry Dane Brimmer. Honesdale, PA: Calkins Creek, 2017.

GRADES 5–8.

Photos and text document this event in which thirteen black and white civil rights activists travel by Greyhound and Trailways buses from Washington, DC, to New Orleans to commemorate the seventh anniversary of *Brown v. Board of Education*. They also intend to test the segregated bus waiting rooms along the way. When they reach Alabama, they are subjected to violence from the Ku Klux Klan: the riders are beaten, and the bus is torched. The extreme violence brings national attention to the cause.

Turning 15 on the Road to Freedom: My Story of the 1965 Selma Voting Rights March. Lynda Blackmon Lowery. As told to Elspeth Leacock and Susan Buckley. Illustrated by PJ Loughran. New York: Dial, 2015.
GRADES 5–8.

The Selma Marches for Voting Rights always included a lot of young people. Lynda Blackmon is arrested and jailed nine times before the historic 1965 march from Selma to Birmingham. She is only fourteen when she embarks on that march, turning fifteen on the road. Her voice feels authentic in this account, which should resonate with young people today.

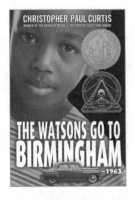

The Watsons Go to Birmingham—1963. Christopher Paul Curtis. New York: Delacorte, 1995.
GRADES 5–8.

It starts as a family trip from Flint, Michigan, to Alabama to visit relatives. Ten-year-old Kenny, little sister Joetta, and thirteen-year-old Byron are typical kids—bickering, complaining, and joking around at times. Things turn dark on a Sunday morning when a large boom comes from the nearby church where black families, including the Watsons, have gathered. The church has been bombed. Kenny sees the bodies of four little girls who look just like his sister Joetta being taken from the church. He feels guilty for having left her alone in the church even though she has not been hurt. It takes time and the love and understanding of his family to recover from the trauma. Introduce children who have read this novel to nonfiction accounts of the Birmingham church bombing, such as *When the Children Marched* by Robert H. Mayer (listed below).

We March. Shane Evans. New York: Roaring Brook Press, 2012.
GRADES K–3.

An African American family takes a bus to Washington, DC, to participate in the March on Washington for Jobs and Freedom in 1963, where 250,000 people gathered to hear Dr. Martin Luther King Jr. give his famous "I Have a Dream" speech. Young readers will need the information in the author's note at the end of the book to understand the context of this journey, but the very simple text and striking illustrations capture the optimism and hope of the march.

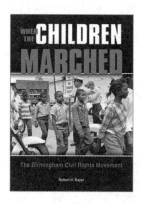

When the Children Marched: The Birmingham Civil Rights Movement. Robert H. Mayer. Berkeley Heights, NJ: Enslow Publishers, 2008.
GRADES 5–8.

Young people played an active role in all the major civil rights initiatives in the South. However, in Birmingham, Alabama, they were the primary participants. When the Reverend Fred Shuttlesworth invites the Southern Christian Leadership Conference (SCLC) to come to the city to help with integration efforts, leaders of the movement make a conscious decision to put children at the forefront of their marches. As a result, hundreds of children—some as young as six—are arrested and jailed in 1962 and 1963. Sheriff Bull Connor's police officers are photographed turning fire hoses and dogs on the children. Some people are critical of Dr. Martin Luther King Jr. and the SCLC leaders for putting the children in danger, but others acknowledge that those dramatic photos have gained the attention of the nation. The marches continue, and the violent reaction to them from the police and militant segregationists escalates. In September 1963, the 16th Street Baptist Church is bombed; four little black girls are killed. In 1964, Congress passes the Civil Rights Act, which includes many of the goals sought by the Birmingham protesters. The Voting Rights Act of 1965 is the next milestone.

Witness to Freedom: Young People Who Fought for Civil Rights.
Belinda Rochelle. New York: Dutton/Lodestar, 1993.
GRADES 5–8.

This book profiles nine African American children and teens who participated in different civil rights marches, protests, and demonstrations. The profiles mention lesser-known incidents, such as the 1951 effort to integrate the R. R. Moton High

School in Farmville, Virginia, as well as the lunch counter sit-ins, *Brown v. Board of Education*, the Montgomery bus boycott, and other landmark events of the civil rights movement.

The Youngest Marcher: The Story of Audrey Faye Hendricks, a Young Civil Rights Activist. Cynthia Levinson. Illustrated by Vanessa Brantley Newton. New York: Atheneum, 2017.
GRADES 2–4.

This picture-book account of the Children's Crusade led by Dr. Martin Luther King Jr. in Birmingham, Alabama, in 1963, focuses on Audrey Faye Hendricks. Nine years old, she is the youngest marcher. Like the other children who are arrested, she spends seven days in juvenile detention. And like those children, she is proud that her efforts call national attention to the cause of civil rights and result in laws that make segregation in public places illegal.

The Environment

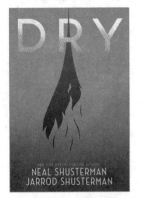

Dry. Neal Shusterman and Jarrod Shusterman. New York: Simon & Schuster, 2018.
GRADES 9 AND UP.

The drought has been a fact of life in Southern California for a long time, but now the taps have run completely dry. Sixteen-year-old Alyssa's parents have gone to look for water and haven't returned. Neighbor is beginning to turn against neighbor when Alyssa, her little brother, and the teenage son of the survivalist family next door set off in search of her parents. Along the way, they meet up with two other teens and negotiate their way through an increasingly violent world in which people are beginning to die from lack of water. This survival story will resonate for the many teenagers of today who see climate change as our single biggest issue.

Earth Feeling the Heat. Brenda Z. Guiberson. Illustrated by Chad Wallace. New York: Henry Holt, 2010.
GRADES K–3.

Beautiful oil paintings and a rhyming text communicate the effect of global warming on various animals. In addition to the narrative, a map shows the habitat of each animal in the text and suggestions for ways that children can help conserve the environment.

Earth in the Hot Seat: Bulletins from a Warming World. Marfe Ferguson
Delano. New York: National Geographic, 2009.
GRADES 5 AND UP.

Presents the evidence for global warming in a straightforward, accessible manner.
This book is clear about what humans have done to contribute to this situation and
offers strategies for averting the worst possible consequences. The research is
impeccable, the message unmistakable and convincing.

Gaia Warriors: Urgent: The Fight Is On! Nicola Davies.
Somerville, MA: Candlewick, 2011.
GRADES 5 AND UP.

The Gaia warriors are activists who are fighting climate
change. Many of them are profiled here: scientists, celebrities, and ordinary young people. Useful information is
presented in an appealing format.

***The Help Yourself Cookbook for Kids: 60+ Easy Plant-Based Recipes Kids
Can Make to Stay Healthy and Save the World.*** Ruby Roth. Kansas City, MO:
Andrews McMeel Publishing, 2016.
GRADES 4 AND UP.

Here is an appealing cookbook for kids who have chosen to be vegan because of
environmental concerns. In addition to providing easy recipes for drinks, sauces,
dips, salads, entrees, and desserts, the author includes a list of ingredients that
might not be as familiar: agave, algae, mocha, nutritional yeast, and so on. There is
also a list of sources for some products that might not be readily available at local
grocery stores.

How the Ladies Stopped the Wind. Bruce McMillan. Illustrated by Gunnella.
Boston: Houghton Mifflin, 2007.

A group of indomitable old ladies in Iceland figure out how to get the chickens to
stop eating their saplings so the trees they plant will grow tall enough to stop the
fierce winds that blow across their country. Use this with Jen Cullerton Johnson's
Seeds of Change (listed later in this section) as part of a booktalk with second and
third graders about environmental issues.

John Muir: My Life with Nature. Joseph Cornell. Nevada City, CA: Dawn
Publications, 2000.
GRADES 4–6.

This is a retelling of Muir's autobiography with black-and-white sketches and photographs to illustrate his life. Cornell explains that he uses Muir's own words as

much as possible, and certainly Muir's love and respect for the natural world shines through. This is an appropriate introduction to the life and work of the man who is known as the Father of American National Parks, the founder of the Sierra Club, and an influential advocate for the preservation of nature.

Kids Care! 75 Ways to Make a Difference for People, Animals and the Environment. Rebecca Olien. Illustrated by Michael Kline. Nashville: Williamson Publications, 2007.
GRADES 2–5.

Much of the focus in this book is on the ways children can demonstrate their empathy and concern for people, other animals, and the environment. Many of the suggested activities would be best accomplished by individuals. However, the last chapter, "Kids Join Together," is full of practical ideas for organizing collective efforts.

Leaf Jumpers. Carole Gerber. Illustrated by Leslie Evans. Watertown, MA: Charlesbridge, 2004.
GRADES PRE-K–2.

This picture book celebrates the change of weather in the fall and the simple pleasure of jumping in the fallen leaves. If the children's attention span allows, use in a preschool or family storytime along with Clyde Bulla's *A Tree is a Plant* (listed later in this section) or H. Joseph Hopkins's *The Tree Lady* (listed later in this section).

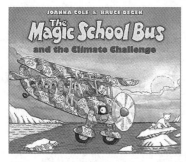

The Magic School Bus and the Climate Challenge. Joanna Cole and Bruce Degen. New York: Scholastic, 2010.
GRADES 2–4.

Ms. Frizzle takes her class to the Arctic to see firsthand how much ice has melted since their outdated textbooks were printed. They learn the planet's climate is changing mostly because of human activity. When they learn that using alternative energy might help, they go check out windmills and generators that operate without using fossil fuels. The children are inspired to make changes by conserving, recycling, and lobbying their elected officials for better policies and practices.

Mama Miti: Wangari Maathi and the Trees of Kenya. Donna Jo Napoli.
Illustrated by Kadir Nelson. New York: Simon & Schuster, 2010.
GRADES K–3.

A simple narrative and stunning oil paintings introduce young readers to the life
and work of the Kenyan woman whose tree-planting campaign earned her the
Nobel Peace Prize. See also *Seeds of Change* by Jen Cullerton Johnson for slightly
older children.

Me . . . Jane. Patrick McDonnell. New York: Little
Brown, 2011.
GRADES PRE-K–2.

Here is a simple story about a little girl named
Jane who loves her toy chimpanzee Jubilee and
loves watching birds, animals, and insects and
learning all she can about them. She reads a story
about another girl named Jane, one who lived with
the apes in Africa and dreamed about doing the
same. The last page is a photograph of the grown-up Jane with a small chimpanzee,
showing that her dream came true. The author's note provides more information
about the life of Jane Goodall and her mission to raise awareness about the plight
of the chimpanzees and about environmental conservation. Maybe this book will
inspire others to follow their dreams to a life of activism. A Caldecott Honor Book.

No One Is Too Small to Make a Difference. Greta Thunberg. Great Britain:
Penguin Random House UK, 2019.
GRADES 7 AND UP.

Greta Thunberg, of course, is the young Swedish climate activist who proudly pro-
claims that Asperger's syndrome helps her see the world clearly. This is a collection
of eleven of her speeches given between September 2018 and April 2019, in which
she challenges adult decision makers to save the world before it is too late. She cites
impressive scientific facts about climate change and the mass extinction of species
and also refutes many of the false statements made about her and her campaign.

Rain! Linda Ashman. Illustrated by Christian Robinson. Boston: Houghton Mifflin
Harcourt, 2013.
GRADES PRE-K–2.

A rainy day makes an old man grumpy, but a little boy loves playing in the sidewalk
puddles. Use this in a family storytime about climate change to show the pleasures
we get from weather.

Red Leaf, Yellow Leaf. Lois Ehlert. New York: Harcourt Brace, 1991.
GRADES PRE-K–3.

A young child explores the beauty and wonder of a maple tree in autumn. There is additional botanical information for a child who wants to know more and guidelines for planting your own tree. Use in a preschool or family storytime about environmental issues along with Clyde Bulla's *A Tree Is a Plant* (listed on the following page) or H. Joseph Hopkins's *The Tree Lady* (listed on the following page).

Sally Goes to the Beach. Stephen Huneck. New York: Abrams, 2000.
GRADES PRE-K–2.

Sally, a black Labrador retriever, has a great day at the beach. Use this along with nonfiction titles at a family storytime about global warming to start a conversation about how weather affects us.

Seeds of Change. Jen Cullerton Johnson. Illustrated by Sonia Lynn Sadler. New York: Lee and Low, 2010.
GRADES 3–5.

Picture-book biography of Wangari Maathai, the Kenyan woman who defied the norms and expectations of her Kikuyu village and became a United States–educated scientist. When she returns to her country, she is appalled at the extent of damage that deforestation has done to the land. She begins a campaign of tree planting, implemented primarily by women throughout Kenya. In a few years they plant more than thirty million trees and attract the negative attention of foreign business interests. Some businessmen bribe corrupt police officers to arrest her. When she is finally released, Maathai's travels take her environmental message to the rest of her country and to the world. She is elected to the Kenya parliament and receives the Nobel Peace Prize in 2004. What a role model! See also *Mama Miti: Wangari Maathi and the Trees of Kenya* by Donna Jo Napoli (listed on the previous page) for younger children.

The Snowy Day. Ezra Jack Keats. New York: Viking, 1962.
GRADES PRE-K–2.

This classic picture book captures the joy of a little boy's day in the snow. Share it at a family storytime with a global warming theme to remind people of the climate we need to work to keep.

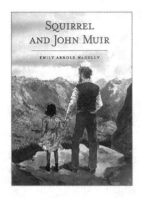

Squirrel and John Muir. Emily Arnold McCully. New York: Farrar, Straus and Giroux, 2004.

GRADES 2–4.

In 1868, John Muir wanders into Yosemite Valley and gets a position doing odd jobs for James Hutchings, who owns a hotel and organizes tours of the area. Floy Hutchings, known as Squirrel, is a spunky girl who loves living in that beautiful unspoiled wilderness. McCully creates a fictional story about a friendship between John Muir and Squirrel, two people who are both passionate about nature. An author's note and a bibliography of adult resources provide background; McCully's illustrations convey the beauty of Yosemite. Adults might want to be aware of possible controversy about Muir's role in removing native tribes from Yosemite. There is no mention of this aspect of his legacy in this book—just his passion for preserving natural beauty.

Tell Me, Tree: All about Trees for Kids. Gail Gibbons. New York: Little, Brown, 2002.

GRADES K–3.

The author provides a lot of basic information in her trademark style: direct, accessible, appealing, and easy to read. Recommended as a companion to *Seeds of Change* by Jen Cullerton Johnson (listed on the previous page).

A Tree Is a Plant. Clyde Bulla. Illustrated by Stacey Schuettl. New York: HarperCollins, 2001.

GRADES K–3.

Everything a young child wants to know about the life cycle of an apple tree is presented in an easy-to-read, attractive book. This is part of the Let's-Read-and-Find-Out Science series. Use this in a booktalk about environmental activism along with *Seeds of Change* by Jen Cullerton Johnson (listed on the previous page).

The Tree Lady: The True Story of How One Tree-Loving Woman Changed a City Forever. H. Joseph Hopkins. Illustrated by Jill McElmurry. New York: Beach Lane Books, 2014.

GRADES 2–4.

When Katherine Olivia Sessions was growing up in Northern California, she loved getting her hands dirty as she gathered needles in the redwood and pine groves there. In 1881 she became the first woman to graduate from the University of California with a degree in science. Arriving in San Diego for her first job, she was surprised to find it a desert almost devoid of trees. She set about to change that, scouring the world for drought-resistant plants that would thrive in the arid soil and dry climate of that city. She started a plant nursery in City Park and organized squads of volunteers to plant trees by the hundreds. Her work transformed San Diego, especially City Park—now called Balboa Park—from a desert landscape to city that is lush with many varieties of trees and shrubs.

True Green Kids: 100 Things You Can Do to Save the Planet. Kim McKay and Jenny Bonnin. Sydney, Australia: ABC Books, 2008. GRADES 2–5.

Here are many easy things that almost any kid could do to help save the environment. Most can be accomplished with little or no money, although adults might have to chip in some cash to buy a solar-powered battery charger. More typical of the suggestions here are using a bucket to capture rainwater, using a timer to limit showers to four minutes, writing to politicians and celebrities to encourage them to be more responsible for the environment, and avoiding single-use plastic bottles. This is an Australian publication, and some of the references are specific to that country; but American children should be able to implement almost all of these ideas.

Untamed: The Wild Life of Jane Goodall. Anita Silvey. Washington, DC: National Geographic, 2015.
GRADES 3–6.

Maps, color photos, and interesting sidebars all add to this biography of Jane Goodall, the scientist best known for her intimate research into the chimpanzees of Gombe in Tanzania. Goodall's activism for the causes of environmental conservation and peace is also acknowledged. In a foreword, Goodall encourages young people to join Roots & Shoots, an organization that enables children and teens to work to save the natural world.

Who Will Plant a Tree? Jerry Pallotta. Illustrated by Tom Leonard. Ann Arbor, MI: Sleeping Bear Press, 2010.
GRADES PRE-K–2.

This book situates trees in many different habitats and demonstrates in an easy text and informative pictures the complex interactions of plants and animals. Introduce this to children along with Jen Cullerton Johnson's *Seeds of Change* (listed earlier in this section).

Why Are Ice Caps Melting? The Dangers of Global Warming. Anne Rockwell. Illustrated by Paul Meisel. New York: Collins, 2006.
GRADES 2–4.

This Stage 2 entry in the Let's-Read-and-Find-Out Science series aims to explain the complex concept of global warming to students in primary grades. It gives the evidence for global warming and explains its causes. It doesn't offer unreasonable optimism about reversing this trend; instead, it offers suggestions of things children can do: plant trees, write letters to elected officials urging them to take the matter seriously, decrease use of electrical appliances, recycle, and learn as much as they can about climate change.

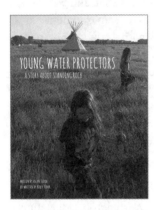

Young Water Protectors: A Story about Standing Rock. Aslan Tudor. Scotts Valley, AZ: CreateSpace Independent Publishing, 2018.
GRADES 2–4.

The effort by Native Americans to stop the oil pipeline threatening the water supply is told through the eyes of an eight-year-old child who was there—living in the camp, going to school, and participating in the protest. The book ends with the information that the protest did not succeed in stopping the pipeline but that the fight continues in court.

Gun Control

Gun Control. Steven Otfinoski. New York: Children's Press, 2012.
GRADES 4–6.

This entry in the Cornerstones of Freedom series is a compact account of the United States' long history with firearms and its largely unsuccessful efforts to control them through legislation. Major events—including assassinations and attempted assassinations of presidents and lawmakers as well as the mass shootings by lone gunmen that have become increasingly common—are presented. The author is careful to avoid taking sides but makes clear the passion that this issue generates by advocates and opponents of gun control.

Parkland. Dave Cullen. New York: HarperCollins, 2019.
GRADES 7 AND UP.

The reporter who covered the Columbine tragedy tells the Parkland story through the eyes of the leaders of the protest movement that followed. Some of these young people—Emma Gonzalez and David Hogg—became national figures. Others, such as Jacklyn Corin, worked more behind the scenes, accomplishing heroic feats of organization on the March for Our Lives. Cullen follows them as they struggle to capitalize on the interest generated by the murder of seventeen people at their high school to shape meaningful gun control legislation. They also struggle with their own emotional responses to the event and the inevitable but undesired celebrity attached to a few of them. For many of these teenagers, their activism after the tragedy not only shifted the national debate on gun control, it also was enormously therapeutic for the survivors.

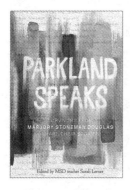

Parkland Speaks: Survivors from Marjory Stoneman Douglas Share Their Stories. Sarah Lerner, editor. New York: Crown, 2019.
GRADES 9–12.

This appealing collection of poetry, drawings, photos, essays, speeches, and firsthand accounts is one of the more accessible publications to come out of the tragedy at Parkland. Since it does not include an overview of the school shooting itself, it requires readers to have that knowledge in advance.

We Say #NeverAgain: Reporting by the Parkland Student Journalists. Melissa Falkowski and Eric Garner, editors. New York: Crown, 2018.
GRADES 10–12/ADULT.

Reporters from all over the world descended on Parkland, Florida, after the mass shooting at Marjory Stoneman Douglas High School. However, the students themselves also reported on the events from their position as insiders and firsthand witnesses to the event. Two high school teachers edited this collection of writing, beginning with accounts from students hidden in classrooms while the shooting is happening to reflections on what the future holds for young people everywhere.

Immigration Issues and Refugees

Dear America: The Story of an Undocumented Citizen. Jose Antonio Vargas. Young Readers' Edition. New York: Harper, 2019.
GRADES 7–9.

Jose is twelve years old when his mother puts him on a plane in the Philippines and sends him to California to live with his grandparents. He doesn't know he is undocumented until he applies for a learner's permit at the Department of Motor Vehicles and the clerk tells him his green card is fake. The story of how he is able to get a scholarship to go to college and find work as a journalist is harrowing. He is lucky in having good friends with the resources to help him, but knowing that he is subject to arrest and deportation at any time takes its toll on his personal and social life. To this day, Vargas continues to write and make films, and he is the founder and CEO of the nonprofit organization Define American, dedicated to securing rights for people like him who lack the documentation to prove that they are American citizens.

Deporting Immigrants. Anne Cunningham, editor. New York: Greenhaven, 2018. GRADES 6 AND UP.

This entry in the Current Controversies series presents two sides to some significant aspects of the immigration issue in the United States. It asks four questions: "Does US immigration policy have its roots in racism?" "Have deportation and immigration policies gotten worse in the new millennium?" "Can deportation in the age of Trump be a boon for America?" "Are immigration and deportation policies headed in the right direction?" An objective overview opens each discussion, which is then followed by pro and con responses. This is an excellent resource for young people forming their own opinions about a national policy with major implications for their own lives, whether they are documented or undocumented citizens.

La Frontera: *El Viaje con Papá / My Journey with Papa.* Deborah Mills and Alfredo Alva. Illustrated by Claudia Navarro. Cambridge, MA: Barefoot Books, 2018. GRADES 3–6.

When it is no longer possible for his father to make a living in their Mexican village, Alfredo joins him on the long, dangerous journey to Texas. The coyote they paid to help does not show up. When they finally arrive in the US as undocumented immigrants, they find shelter in a camp ironically called the Embassy. Alberto starts school with many warnings from his father about what to do if he encounters men in uniform. He begins to learn enough English to get along, but he still misses his mother and siblings back in Mexico. Life gets better when President Ronald Reagan grants amnesty to millions of immigrants, and his father starts the long process of applying for citizenship. It gets even better when the rest of his family joins Alberto and his papa in El Paso, ready to begin a new life together in a new country.

Mama's Nightingale: A Story of Immigration and Separation. Edwige Danticat. Illustrated by Leslie Staub. New York: Dial, 2015.
GRADES K–3.

Haitian-born Edwige Danticat tells a poignant story of a little girl whose undocumented mother was taken from the restaurant where she worked by ICE—or the immigration police, as young Saya calls them. Saya visits her mother weekly but cries every time she has to say goodbye. Her father gives her mother a tape recorder, and she records stories for Saya. Saya's favorite is about a nightingale who goes on long journey but returns to the baby who misses her. This story has a happier ending than that of most families with a loved one detained by ICE: Saya writes a story about her situation that is picked up by the local newspaper and results in a special hearing that frees her mother. An author's note states that more than seventy thousand parents of American-born children have been jailed and deported in recent years. She dedicates this book to those children.

My Family Divided. Diane Guerrero with Erica Moroz. New York: Henry Holt, 2018.
GRADES 7 AND UP.

The author is an actress who has appeared in the television series *Orange Is the New Black* and *Jane the Virgin*. She was born in the US, the child of two undocumented immigrants from Colombia. They were deported when she was a teenager, leaving her to live with family friends. Her father in particular had a hard time adjusting to his situation in Colombia, while her mother eventually moved to Spain and made a better life for herself there. Guerrero, who had always been a performer at heart, took acting classes after college and eventually found herself in New York, going on endless auditions until she got the big role on *Orange Is the New Black*. Her story is about survival as well as the feelings of anger and loss she experienced.

Other Words for Home. Jasmine Warga. New York: HarperCollins, 2019.
GRADES 5–8.

When the civil unrest in Syria becomes too violent and close to home, Jude and her pregnant mother leave to join family in Cincinnati. Jude misses her father and worries about her brother, who is involved in the militant struggle to overthrow the current government. She assumes that their time in the United States is temporary. Over time, however, her English gets better, and she comes to love some aspects of her new school there. She gets a part in the school play and becomes friends with an interesting boy. She starts her period and proudly wears the traditional headscarf of a Muslim woman. When her little sister is born, she begins to realize that this baby is an American and that she is becoming one too. Syria is home; so is her uncle's home in Cincinnati. This is a poignant story that is repeated over and over again as refugees build new lives in new countries while maintaining ties of love and culture and tradition with the old.

Refugees and Migrants. Ceri Roberts. Illustrated by Hanane Kai. Hauppauge, NY: Barrons Educational Series, 2016.
GRADES K–3.

This book does much to give children an understanding of the reasons that families with children and even children on their own decide to immigrate to another country. It also details the hardships and sacrifice that is almost always involved in making such a move as well as the difficulties that migrant and refugee children might have adjusting to their new way of life. This is an excellent source of information and a tool for cultivating tolerance and compassion.

Stepping Stones: A Refugee Family's Journey. Margriet Ruurs. Illustrated by Nizar Ali Badr. Canada: Orca Books, 2016.
GRADES K–3.

Bilingual English-Arabic text. A little girl tells about her life in their old country in the Middle East, where the rooster crows every morning to wake up the family. Where breakfast was bread, yogurt, and tomatoes from their garden. Where she and her brother and her friends played on sunbaked soil. Then war came to the country and food was scarce. Then war came too close to their village, and the family had to leave. They walked and walked until they came to the sea and took a treacherous voyage in a small boat to a land. Then they walked and walked again until they reached a new home where they were welcomed by people who smiled and shared their clothes, food, and even a doll. Unusual illustrations, made by a Syrian sculptor from stones formed to create the people in the story, add dimension to the text.

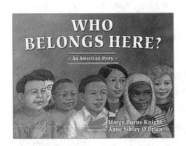

Who Belongs Here? An American Story.
Margy Burns Knight. Illustrated by Anne Sibley O'Brien. Thomaston, ME: Tilbury, 2018.
GRADES 2–4.

Using the true story of a Cambodian boy who immigrated to this country after his parents were killed by the regime of Pol Pot, the author makes the experience of being violently uprooted from home feel real. Sidebars on each page give additional useful information about refugees and immigration. Back matter includes more details about Pol Pot's reign of terror; Dith Pran, a Cambodian photojournalist who raised awareness about geno-cide; Dolores Huerta, the activist who worked on behalf of Mexican farmworkers in this country; the Iroquois Confederacy; and other issues related to refugees and migrants.

Labor Issues

Elegy on the Death of Cesar Chavez. Rudolfo Anaya. Illustrated by Gaspar Enriquez. El Paso, TX: Cinco Puntos Press, 2000.
GRADES 6 AND UP.

This eloquent poem by a well-known Chicano author is a fitting tribute to a hero of the United Farm Workers and an inspiration to the Mexican American community. Anaya includes a note that outlines the contributions of Cesar Chavez for young people who might be unfamiliar with them. Paintings drenched with color and emotion contribute to this beautiful memorial.

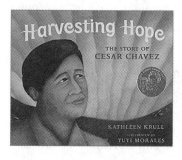

Harvesting Hope: The Story of Cesar Chavez. Kathleen Krull. Illustrated by Yuyi Morales. Boston: Houghton Mifflin, 2003.
GRADES 2–4.

Chavez harvests crops with his parents as a boy and leaves school after eighth grade. As a grown-up, he returns to the California fields and organizes farmworkers to unite for better pay and better working conditions, ultimately found-ing the National Farm Workers Union and winning the first contract for those who labor in the fields. No mention here of his peer Dolores Huerta, unfortunately, but otherwise a beautifully illustrated introduction to an important role model.

Malala, a Brave Girl from Pakistan/Iqbal, a Brave Boy from Pakistan: Two Stories of Bravery. Jeannette Winter. New York: Beach Lane Books, 2014.
GRADES 2–4.

Combines two stories back-to-back. Malala's story is more familiar, and it opens here with the Taliban fighter asking the girls in the school bus: "Who is Malala?" before shooting her. The brief account that follows focuses on her outspoken efforts on behalf of education for girls in Pakistan. Iqbal, the hero of the second story, is less well known to Americans. He was a poor boy indentured to a carpet factory because of a twelve-dollar debt owed by his parents. When he was freed from being literally chained to a loom day after day, he embarked on a campaign to end child labor in his country. Like Malala, he was shot. Unlike her, he did not survive. These are two inspiring stories of children's empowerment in the face of great personal danger.

On Our Way to Oyster Bay: Mother Jones and Her March for Children's Rights. Monica Kulling. Illustrated by Felicita Sala. Tonawanda, NY: Kids Can Press, 2016.
GRADES 2–4.

In 1903, labor activist Mother Jones visits the cotton mill where eight-year-old Aidan is on the picket line with other striking workers. Mother Jones, long active in support of workers' rights, wants to do something dramatic to call attention to the cruelty and injustice of child labor. She decides to organize a children's march from Philadelphia to the summer home of President Theodore Roosevelt in Oyster Bay, New York. Aidan goes along on that march and is disappointed when the president refuses to even meet with the children. Mother Jones tells him not to be discouraged—more people are now aware that children like him who must work to help support their families are also not able to go to school. She is certain that change will come. Back matter tells more about the real historical figure Mother Jones, information about child labor today, and suggestions for children who want to get more involved.

Side by Side: The Story of Dolores Huerta and Cesar Chavez / Lado a Lado: La Historia de Dolores Huerta y Cesar Chavez. Monica Brown. New York: HarperCollins, 2010.
GRADES 3–6.

Bilingual account of the two people responsible for organizing farmworkers in California in order to win better working conditions and pay. Their efforts over a period of more than twenty years win significant victories for farm laborers and even lead to the passage of an immigration act in 1986, which enables a million workers to become United States citizens. "Si, se puede!"

LGBTQIA+ Rights

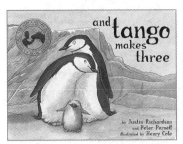

And Tango Makes Three. Justin Richardson and Peter Parnell. Illustrated by Henry Cole. New York: Simon & Schuster, 2005. 10th Anniversary Edition.
GRADES K–3.

Groundbreaking book about the two male penguins in a New York zoo who became a couple and with the help of an observant and ingenious zookeeper became daddies of their own little chick. It has won awards from both the ASPCA and the Lambda Society for its tolerant approach to both animal and gay rights. It has turned out to be an easy way for some parents to introduce their young children to the reality that same-sex couples can be parents and that kids can have two mommies or two daddies as well as the more traditional set.

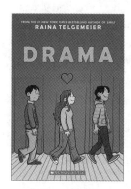

Drama. Raina Telgemeier. New York: Graphix/Scholastic, 2012.

GRADES 6–9.

There is a lot of drama in this graphic novel about a group of eighth graders putting on an ambitious school play. Callie is a theater buff in charge of sets for the play. In between designing and building, she gets a crush on a cute boy—one of a pair of twins. It gets complicated when it turns out that Jesse is gay, and even more complicated when the girl who stars in the play is a no-show for the performance. Jesse astonishes everyone when he knows every line and every song and takes on the role of a Southern belle in a full skirt. Telegemeier is a genius when it comes to writing realistic middle school dialogue, and she captures the range of reactions to Jesse's coming out and his possible first romance with another boy.

Gay & Lesbian History for Kids: The Century-Long Struggle for LGBT Rights.
Jerome Pohlen. Chicago: Chicago Review Press, 2016.
GRADES 6 AND UP.

The book starts with some historical figures who are presumed to have been gay: Plato, Sappho, Michelangelo, and others. The focus, however, is on the most recent hundred years, particularly in the United States. Young readers will learn about gay, lesbian, and bisexual people living in the shadows and about some who were probably transgender before the term was even coined. They can read about the 1960s and '70s, when more and more people came out and won acceptance. Then there was the AIDS crisis of the 1980s and a conservative backlash. The book ends on a positive note with the legalization of gay marriage. This is required reading for LGBTQIA+ kids and their allies.

George. Alex Gino. New York: Scholastic, 2015.
GRADES 3–6.

George knows she's a girl—never mind that her anatomy would indicate differently. She's in the fourth grade, where the boys tease her and her best friend is a girl. When it's time to cast the school play, *Charlotte's Web*, she knows she should be Charlotte. She rehearses the part until she knows it by heart. But the drama teacher thinks her reading is a joke, so George's best friend Kelly gets to play the kind-hearted Charlotte instead. There is an altercation with the boys who bully George that results in a visit to the principal's office. There she sees a poster with a rainbow flag and the words "Support safe spaces for gay, lesbian, bisexual, and transgender youth." George wonders if she will ever find a safe space for girls like her. On the second night of the play, Kelly lets George take her place as Charlotte, and she is a success. Kelly accepts her as a girl, even to the point of helping her dress as a girl for a day at the Bronx Zoo with her uncle. George finally tells her mother, who agrees that maybe they both need some professional help to deal with this reality. This is an important book for young children who feel that they have been trapped in the wrong gender, and for their classmates who could be as big a help as Kelly is to George.

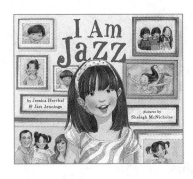

I Am Jazz. Jessica Herthel and Jazz Jennings. Illustrated by Shelagh McNicholas. New York: Dial, 2014.
GRADES K–3.

Jazz tells us about her favorite things: dancing, singing, drawing, swimming, wearing makeup, and pretending she's a pop star. She also tells us that she has a girl's brain in a boy's body. She tells us that when she and her parents learned that she was transgender, they accepted her as a girl and soon most of her classmates did too. It is likely that over time more children will be acknowledged as transgender, and books like this will help them and their friends and family meet them as they are.

Julian Is a Mermaid. Jessica Love. Somerville, MA: Candlewick Press, 2018.
GRADES K–2.

Julian loves everything about being a mermaid. Who says a boy can't be a mermaid? And isn't it wonderful that his grandmother understands and supports him completely?

Pride: The Story of Harvey Milk and the Rainbow Flag. Rob Sanders. Illustrated by Steven Salerno. New York: Random House, 2018.
GRADES 4–6.

When Harvey Milk is elected to the San Francisco Board of Supervisors in 1977, he becomes one of the first openly gay people to hold political office in the United States. He continues his long-standing activism for gay rights in many ways, including organizing marches. It is his idea to have a visible symbol of the movement, so he and artist Gilbert Baker design a rainbow flag. It flies for the first time in the Gay Freedom Pride Parade in San Francisco in 1978. It is then adopted worldwide as a symbol of the gay rights movement. Harvey Milk does not live to see this happen, however—just a few months after that pride parade, he is assassinated, as is Mayor George Moscone. However, the cause lives on— and on June 26, 2015, the US Supreme Court rules that gay couples have the right to get married. On that day, the White House is bathed in lights the color of the rainbow flag.

Nonviolent Protest

Gandhi. Demi. New York: Margaret K. McElderry Books, 2001.

GRADES 2–5.

A brief but very informative biography of this great political and social leader. It gives useful background details that help the reader understand the significance of events such as the Salt March and Gandhi's role in generating a nonviolent movement for Indian independence. Demi's illustrations are a handsome addition to the engaging text.

Gandhi. Leonard Everett Fisher. New York: Atheneum, 1995.
GRADES 3–6.

While this brief biography covers all of Gandhi's life, it gives particular attention to the twenty years he spent in South Africa, where he developed the philosophy and practice of *satyagraha*—a form of nonviolent protest against injustice and oppression that is based on truth and love. Fisher's signature black-and-white illustrations are a dignified and often somber amplification of the text.

Gandhi: The Young Protester Who Founded a Nation. Philip Wilkinson. Washington, DC: National Geographic, 2005.
GRADES 3–6.

This brief biography covers Gandhi's entire life, from his boyhood in a privileged family in Gujarat to his assassination in 1948. The roots of his philosophy of nonviolence are shown, including his mother's reverence for life and his fascination with other world religions. His first nonviolent efforts for social change take place in South Africa, where Indians are discriminated against by the government. Returning to India, he works at first to improve the lot of the untouchable caste and founds an ashram devoted to *satyagraha*, a philosophy and way of life based on nonviolence. The 1929 Salt March is covered in some detail, as is the long, slow political road to India's independence from Britain. Illustrated with many photos and maps.

Peaceful Fights for Equal Rights. Bob Sanders. Illustrated by Jared Andrew Schorr. New York: Simon and Schuster, 2018.
GRADES 2–5.

The deceptively simple text is a catalog of strategies for using peaceful protest to bring about social change. Many of these strategies are not readily available to most children, but seeing them all listed here is inspiring. A sympathetic adult may find this book a useful platform for generating conversation about what children *can* do to make the world a better place. My favorite page: "Read. Remember. Resist."

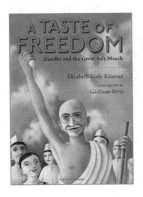

A Taste of Freedom: Gandhi and the Great Salt March. Elizabeth Cody Kimmel. Illustrated by Giuliano Ferri. New York: Walker, 2014.
GRADES 2–5.

A great-grandfather tells a young boy about the time long ago when he was just a boy and joined Mahatma Gandhi on the Great Salt March to the sea from his small inland village. There he listened as Gandhi told the assembled villagers how they will fight the hated British rule with peaceful actions and love. As an old man, he can still remember reaching the sea, taking a pebble of salt, and putting it to his tongue—his first taste of freedom.

Schools

Free as a Bird: The Story of Malala. Lina Maslo. New York: HarperCollins, 2018.
GRADES 1–3.

The picture-book biography of Malala Yousafzai focuses on her relationship with her father and his influence on her activism for the education of girls. An author's note and timeline are helpful for filling in some important background—including the rise of the Taliban after the devastating 2005 earthquake in Pakistan—as well as clarifying how Malala ended up in the hospital in England after being shot in the head.

Hector: A Boy, a Protest, and the Photograph that Changed Apartheid.
Adrienne Wright. Salem, MA: Page Street, 2019.
GRADES 2–5.

When the South African government decrees that all black students be taught half of their subjects in Afrikaans instead of English, young people and their parents begin to resist apartheid in earnest. This is the story of one student protest in Soweto in 1976 that turns deadly. It starts as an ordinary day for twelve-year-old Hector. On his way to school, he encounters the students from the high school who are protesting the new law. He is swept up in the excitement. Police begin shooting, and he is killed. A teenage boy picks him up to take him off the street; a photographer captures the moment. That photo (reproduced in the book) is seen worldwide and helps turn public sentiment against the South African regime and its policy of apartheid. Author's notes at the beginning and end of the book will contextualize this event for American children who may not be familiar with it.

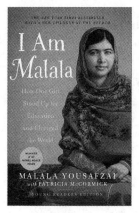

I Am Malala: How One Girl Stood Up for Education and Changed the World. Malala Yousafzai with Patricia McCormick. New York: Little, Brown, 2014.
GRADES 5–8.

This Young Reader Edition is written from Malala's point of view as a young Pakistani girl growing up in a family that encourages her education—an unusual situation for girls in that time and place. Much credit is given to her father in particular, who encourages her to write and speak publicly about the need for universal education at a time when Pakistani leaders are under the influence of Islamic extremists and denying girls' access to schools. It is clear that she knew from a very early age that she has special talents and a special destiny. She was well known before the shooting that nearly killed her in 2012, but this event propelled her to world attention. Her persistence in advocating for girls' rights to education, even after moving with her family to Birmingham, England, for their safety, won her the Nobel Prize for Peace in 2014.

Malala: A Hero for All. Shana Corey. Illustrated by Elizabeth Sayles. New York: Random House, 2016.
GRADES 2–3.

This leveled reader from the Step into Reading series opens with Malala speaking to the United Nations and then tells the true story of how she got there. The language and content are appropriate for the seven- and eight-year-olds who are the intended readers, giving just enough geographical and political background for context. While Malala's father is given much credit for empowering her to speak up for girls' education, her mother is also portrayed as a significant influence through acts of generosity to less fortunate people.

Malala: Activist for Girls' Education. Raphaële Frier. Illustrated by Aurelia Fronty. Watertown, MA: Charlesbridge, 2015.
GRADES 2–4.

The text makes clear how Malala's family encourages her to think about the bigger issues facing her country and to have the courage and confidence to speak up when the Taliban forbids girls to go to school in Pakistan. It also tells how she expands her crusade on behalf of girls' education to other parts of the world after receiving the Nobel Prize. Significant back matter provides additional information about Pakistan, education for girls, Islam, and Malala's sources of inspiration, such as Gul Makai, Gandhi, Nelson Mandela, and Dr. Martin Luther King Jr. Also features a useful list of resources for more information.

Malala's Magic Pencil. Malala Yousafzai. Illustrated by Kerascoët. New York: Little, Brown, 2017.
GRADES K–3.

This picture-book autobiography of Malala tells the story of her life and achievements in words and pictures—more are accessible to younger children than her longer biography, I Am Malala.

The Power of One: Daisy Bates and the Little Rock Nine. Judith Bloom Fradin and Dennis Brindell Fradin. New York: Clarion, 2004.
GRADES 5–8.

As a child, Daisy Bates experiences firsthand the hateful effects of race-based segregation. Her father counsels her on his deathbed to stop hating white people and to start hating discrimination and prejudice. Only then can she change things. She takes his words to heart. After marrying newspaper publisher L. C. Bates, she works with him to promote civil rights and becomes the chair of the Arkansas NAACP. It is in this capacity that she becomes involved with the nine black teenagers who integrated Little Rock Central High School in an unusually fraught and violent environment. While this book focuses on her contributions to that event, it also offers a lot of behind-the-scenes information about the young people who were on the front lines.

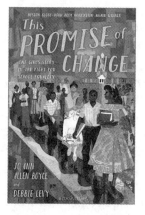

The Promise of Change: One Girl's Story in the Fight for School Equality. Jo Ann Allen Boyce and Debbie Levy. New York: Bloomsbury, 2019. GRADES 5–8.

It is 1956, and the United States Supreme Court has ruled four years before in *Brown v. Board of Education* that separate schools for black and white children are inherently unequal and deprive black children of the equal protection of the law guaranteed by the Fourteenth Amendment. It has taken two more years for the small town of Clinton, Tennessee, to admit black students to its public high school. This memoir in verse recounts the experience of Jo Ann Allen, one of the twelve black teenagers who enter the formerly all-white high school that year. They are greeted with insults, isolation, and enough violence that Jo Ann's parents decide to leave for better opportunities in California after she endures just one semester. Only six black students stick it out for that entire school year and go on to graduate from Clinton High. In spite of what must have seemed like a failure for the brave teenagers who were on the front lines of that integration battle, Jo Ann recalls her feeling of pride and victory when not one white supremacist segregationist who ran for mayor or alderman that December won. "Before all this, / before all that happened / happened, I thought there was nothing I could do / about segregation. / I'm just a girl, I thought, / one girl who tries / to look at the good side of things, / because there's nothing I can do / about the bad. / I'm still that good-side-looking girl, / but now when I see the bad, I'll think— / *I'll know*— / there's something I can do about it" (233). This is a moving account of courage and resilience (and "stubbornness," Jo Ann would add) that is often needed when a few activists face great odds to effect needed change.

Ruby Bridges Goes to School: My True Story. Ruby Bridges. New York: Scholastic, 2009.
GRADES 1–2.

Here is Ruby Bridges's story simplified for beginning readers. The content and accompanying photos are well chosen. This is a good introduction to the subject of racial segregation in this country and to one little black girl's firsthand experience in overturning the practice in New Orleans. See also *Through My Eyes* by Bridges, later in this section.

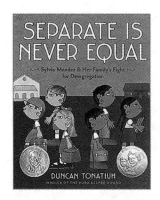

Separate Is Never Equal: Sylvia Mendez and Her Family's Fight for Desegregation. Duncan Tonatiuh. New York: Abrams, 2014.
GRADES 2–4.

Not at all as familiar as *Brown vs. Board of Education*, the Mendez family's efforts seven years before resulted in the desegregation of all public schools in California. Like Ruby Bridges, Sylvia Mendez is one of the first Mexican children to attend a previously segregated public school in Westminster. This illustrated nonfiction account focuses more on her father's initiative and leadership in launching the lawsuit that accomplishes it, but Sylvia's experiences in the inferior Mexican school and in the newly integrated school are documented as well. Sibert Honor Book and Pura Belpré Honor Book.

The Story of Ruby Bridges. Robert Coles. Illustrated by George Ford. New York: Scholastic, 1995.
GRADES K–3.

Picture-book account of Ruby Bridges's experience as the first black child to start first grade at an integrated public school in New Orleans. Written by the prominent psychologist who studied and counseled Ruby and her family during the integration effort, it depicts a little girl whose faith in God enables her to face crowds of hate-filled white adults with courage and dignity and forgiveness.

Today the World Is Watching You: The Little Rock Nine and the Fight for School Integration 1957. Kekla Magoon. Minneapolis: Lerner/Twenty-First Century Books, 2011.
GRADES 5–9.

Like the story of Ruby Bridges in New Orleans, this is another account of courageous and committed young people, with the support of the NAACP and other concerned adults, who defied the segregationist school board and Arkansas governor in order to integrate Central High School in Little Rock. Their efforts require the intervention of President Dwight Eisenhower, who sends the National Guard to protect the nine black students from violence at the hands of white adults and students. While the militant segregationists are a minority of Little Rock residents, their extreme tactics bring national and worldwide attention to the issue and delay meaningful integration for the entire school year. It is a horrendous experience for the Little Rock Nine. One of them is expelled for standing up to harassment from white students; others leave because the disruption interferes too much with their schooling. Only three of them stayed on to graduate from Central High. Ultimately, however, all nine graduate from college and go on to have productive adult lives. The author provides useful background information about racism and segregation in the United States and about the legal procedures that resulted in the Supreme Court decision banning "separate but equal" schools for black and white children. Back matter includes a detailed timeline, biographical information about the Little Rock Nine and other significant figures, and suggestions for further research.

Todos Iguales: Un Corrido de Lemon Grove / All Equal: A Ballad of Lemon Grove. Christy Hale. New York: Children's Book Press, 2019.
GRADES 3–5.

Before there was *Brown v. Board of Education of Topeka* or *Mendez v. Westminster School District of Orange County*, there was *Roberto Alvarez v. Board of Trustees of the Lemon Grove School District*, the first successful school desegregation case in the United States. Roberto Alvarez is a twelve-year-old student at the Lemon Grove School, where white and Mexican American children are both enrolled. When the school board decides to open a segregated and inferior school for its Mexican American students, his parents and others in the community file a successful lawsuit. Robert's poised testimony in court does much to disprove the school board's argument that the Mexican American children are backward and in need of remedial education.

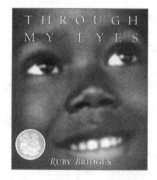

Through My Eyes. Ruby Bridges. New York: Scholastic, 1999.
GRADES 3–5.

Bridges's own account of the experience of being the lone six-year-old black child charged with integrating her public school in 1960. Contemporary photographs and quotes from news articles and interviews will help children of today understand the importance and the force of that event. Much is made of Ruby's bravery as she faces crowds of angry white people who throw rocks and eggs and yell vile obscenities at her. The adult Bridges downplays her own courage and gives much credit to her uprising by a strict mother and by her own faith in the power of prayer. This is an empowering, inspirational book that should be widely shared with all our children. See also *Ruby Bridges Goes to School: My True Story*, earlier in this section.

Voting Rights for Women

Alice Paul and the Fight for Women's Rights.
Deborah Kops. Honesdale, PA: Calkins Press, 2017.
GRADES 6–9.

Alice Paul is not as well-known as older suffragists such as Susan B. Anthony and Elizabeth Cady Stanton, but she was an important leader of the early women's movement. Born in 1885 and raised a Quaker, she is drawn to the cause of women's suffrage as a young woman going to school in England. She is arrested for the first time in 1909 at a demonstration led by Emmeline Pankhurst. Returning to the United States, she is at the forefront of the fight with Congress for a constitutional amendment that would guarantee women the right to vote. Much of this book documents the political infighting and strategizing that finally leads to the passage of the Nineteenth Amendment in 1920. She doesn't stop her efforts with that victory but spends the rest of her life working for equal rights for women. She is credited with writing the Equal Rights Amendment, which still has not been ratified. The author makes the point that even though that amendment has not passed, many of its provisions have come to pass, such as Title IX, which prohibits any school that discriminates on the basis of sex from receiving federal funds. This has had an enormous positive effect on women's athletics.

Around America to Win the Vote: Two Suffragists, a Kitten, and 10,000 Miles. Mara Rockliff. Somerville, MA: Candlewick, 2016.
GRADES 2–5.

True story of two women who drove their little yellow car from New York to California and back in a campaign to win the vote for women in 1916. They faced bad roads, bad weather, and a scarcity of maps and directions, but succeeded. Author's notes emphasize what a feat this was in those early days of the automobile, and also give a brief history of the American suffrage movement that finally won the vote for women in 1920.

Elizabeth Started All the Trouble. Doreen Rappaport. Illustrated by Matt Faulkner. New York: Disney-Hyperion, 2016.
GRADES 2–4.

Excellent introduction to the women's suffrage movement. The author contextualizes the struggle by starting with Abigail Adams's words to her husband, John, who was with his other male friends drafting the United States Constitution: "Don't forget the ladies." It took more than 230 years for American women to have the right to vote, even after Lincoln emancipated the slaves. The author gives space to some of the lesser-known women who played important roles in the struggle: the Grimke sisters, Lucy Stone, Amelia Bloomer, and others, as well as leaders like Elizabeth Cady Stanton, Susan B. Anthony, Lucretia Mott, and Sojourner Truth. The picture-book format makes this an appealing overview of an important episode in American history and gives young women in particular some admirable role models.

Heart on Fire: Susan B. Anthony Votes for President. Ann Malaspina. Illustrated by Steve James. Chicago: Albert Whitman, 2012. GRADES 2–4.

In 1868, Congress ratifies the Fourteenth Amendment to free black slaves. However, Susan B. Anthony and other suffragettes further interpret it to give full rights of citizenship to women, including the right to vote. In 1872, with the presidential election four days away, Susan B. Anthony registers to vote. On Election Day, November 5, she and fifteen other women show up to vote. On November 18, she is arrested by a deputy federal marshal for "voting without having the lawful right to vote." In June 1879, she is tried and convicted. However, she refuses to pay one cent of her fine. This is an accessible, easy-to-read account of that event that was one of many acts of civil disobedience used by women to call attention to their cause and eventually win the right to vote in 1920.

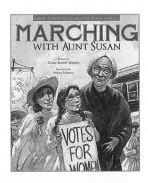

Marching with Aunt Susan: Susan B. Anthony and the Fight for Women's Suffrage. Claire Rudolf Murphy. Illustrated by Stacey Schuett. Atlanta, GA: Peachtree, 2011. GRADES 2–4.

It is 1894 in Berkeley, California, and ten-year-old Bessie wants to go hiking with her dad. She is told that strenuous exercise is not ladylike. Instead, she must stay home and help her mother and her aunt prepare for a suffrage tea, where the guest of honor will be Susan B. Anthony. Later she hears Ms. Anthony—known to everybody in the movement as Aunt Susan—speak at a huge rally. Bessie is inspired by the message that girls are as good as boys and can do anything that boys can do. She and her friend work in the suffrage office and go on marches to try to convince the men in California to extend voting rights to women. That effort fails, but her father agrees to take her hiking the next weekend. Back matter and an author's note give a brief biography of Susan B. Anthony and a timeline of events leading to women's suffrage in 1920. The character Bessie is based on a real girl whom the author discovered in papers at the Bancroft Library.

Conclusion

A recent health policy brief from the California Endowment argues that civic engagement by young people—volunteering, voting, and participating in school and community organizations—promotes healthy youth development. It does this by contributing to a sense of self-efficacy, by increasing leadership and communication skills, and by providing access to resources and services. The policy brief also notes that rates of civic engagement by teens differ. Teens from higher-income families are more likely to volunteer than those from lower-income families. Youth of color are also less likely to have opportunities for civic engagement (Babey and Wolstein 2018). Regardless of race, ethnicity, or socioeconomic status, all children and teens deserve access to such opportunities.

These findings suggest more than a reason for public libraries to fill the opportunity gap. These findings are a mandate, a call to action. The latest research as reported in the health policy brief indicates that civic engagement is not just a way for teens to meet a graduation requirement for community service or to make a contribution to their neighborhoods. It is actually an important determinant of their own health and welfare.

Those of us who study and work in public libraries have come to understand that our mission to young people is a broad one. Yes, we are there to provide books and information. Yes, we are there to provide opportunities to learn and use the latest technologies. Yes, we are there to help young people develop their personal and social skills by participating in advisory boards and volunteer activities. More broadly, however, the public library is an important node in a network of community supports for children and teens. As stated by Nicole

Yohalem and Karen Pittman (2003), two youth advocates who worked with the Public Libraries as Partners in Youth Development initiative: when communities support young people, the young people in return contribute to the community. Public libraries can be an important part of this circle of support.

Children and YA librarians value their young patrons not just for the adults they are growing up to be, but for the smart, funny, interesting, valuable human beings they are today and for the contributions they make to their communities. I concluded another book I wrote for the American Library Association, *Twenty-First Century Kids, Twenty-First Century Librarians*, with two lines from *The Surrender Tree*, a novel in verse by Margarita Engle (2008, 133):

> Young people drift on airy daydreams.
> Old folks help hold them in place.

To me, those lines exemplify the opportunities and support we can offer the children and teens we serve in our public libraries. We give them the chance to soar by introducing them to life-changing books and ideas as well as avenues to contribute to their communities. And we act as anchors, providing a foundation and a focus for their dreams. How fortunate we are to have found a profession that allows us to do all of that.

References

ALA American Library Association and Harwood Institute for Public Innovation. *Community Conversation Workbook*. n.d. Chicago: American Library Association and the Harwood Institute for Public Innovation. Accessed November 13, 2019. Ala.org.

Alessio, Amy, ed. *Excellence in Library Service to Young Adults*. 2008. 5th ed. Chicago: American Library Association / Young Adult Library Services Association.

Astor, Maggie. 2018. "Speakers, Students, Activists, Survivors." *New York Times*, August 16, 2018, A11.

Babey, Susan H., and Joelle Wolstein. 2018. *Civic Engagement among California High School Teens*. Los Angeles: UCLA Center for Health Policy Research.

Benton Foundation. *Buildings, Books, and Bytes: Libraries and Communities in the Digital Age*. 1996. Washington, DC: Benton Foundation/Kellogg Foundation.

Blitzer, Jonathan. 2019. "The Trump Administration's Plot to End DACA Faces a Supreme Court Test." *New Yorker*, November 10, 2019.

Bodart, Joni Richards, ed. 1993. *Booktalk! 5 More Selections from The Booktalker for All Ages and Audiences*. New York: H. W. Wilson.

Braverman, Miriam. 1979. *Youth, Society, and the Public Library*. Chicago: American Library Association.

Center for Civic Education. 2003. *National Standards for Civics and Government*. Calabasas, CA: Center for Civic Education.

Clay, Andreana. 2012. *The Hip-Hop Generation Fights Back: Youth, Activism, and Post–Civil Rights Politics.* New York: New York University Press.

Coles, Robert. 1986. *The Political Life of Children.* Boston: Atlantic Monthly Press.

Easton, David, and Jack Dennis. 1969. *Children in the Political System: Origins of Political Legitimacy.* New York: McGraw-Hill.

Engle, Margarita. 2008. *The Surrender Tree: Poems of Cuba's Struggle.* New York: Holt.

Francisco, Grace, Kathryn Covier Hannah, Shelly G. Keller, Joan Waters, and Patricia M. Y. Wong. 2001. *Joint Ventures: The Promise, Power and Performance of Partnerships.* Sacramento: California State Library.

Greenstein, Fred I. 1969. *Children and Politics.* New Haven, CT: Yale University Press.

Gross, Melissa. 1995. "The Imposed Query." RQ [*Reference & User Services Quarterly*] 35, no. 2 (Winter 1995): 126–243.

Hussey, Kristin. 2018. "Emboldened by Parkland, Newtown Students Find Voice." *New York Times*, August 27, 2018, A23.

Jarvie, Jenny. 2018. "Balancing Homework and Changing the World: Students' March Aims to 'Wake Up' Congress." *Los Angeles Times*, March 23, 2018, A1, A14.

Koester, Amy. 2019. "A Civic Initiative about Information: The Civic Lab at Skokie Public Library." *Public Libraries*, July/August 2019, 44–52.

Kohli, Sonali. 2019. "High School Kids Focus on Preventing Gun Violence." *Los Angeles Times*, May 27, 2019, B1, B6.

LA Times. "Young Climate Activist Responds to Taunts from Trump, Others." 2019. *Los Angeles Times*, September 28, 2019, A4.

Leigh, Robert D. 1950. *The Public Library in the United States.* New York: Columbia University Press.

Lopez, Steve. 2019. "Tired of Gun Violence." *Los Angeles Times*, November 28, 2019, B1, B6.

McCabe, Ronald. 2001. *Civic Librarianship: Renewing the Social Mission of the Public Library.* Lanham, MD: Scarecrow Press.

Mihailidis, Paul. 2014. *Media Literacy and the Emerging Citizen: Youth, Engagement, and Participation in Digital Culture.* New York: Peter Lang.

Miller, C. 2009. *Service Learning and Civic Efficacy Among Youth with Disabilities.* PhD diss., http://eric.ed.gov/?id=ED532187.

Moeller-Peiffer, Kathleen. "Libraries Invest in Active Shooter Training." 2015. *American Libraries*, June 8, 2015. https://americanlibrariesmagazine.org/ 2015/06/08/libraries-invest-in-active-shooter-training/.

Molz, Redmond Kathleen, and Phyllis Dain. 1999. *Civic Space/Cyberspace: The American Public Library in the Information Age.* Cambridge, MA: MIT Press.

Morgan, Lori A. 2016. "Developing Civic Literacy and Efficacy: Insights Gleaned through the Implementation of Project Citizen." *Inquiry in Education* 8, no. 1, article 3. http://digitalcommons.nl.edu/ie/vol8/iss1/3.

Munson, Amelia H. 1950. *An Ample Field: Books and Young People.* Chicago: American Library Association.

NAMLE National Association for Media Literacy Education. N.d. Media Literacy One Sheet. https://Namle.net.

NASP and NASRO National Association of School Psychologists and National Association of School Resource Officers. 2014. *Best Practice Considerations for Schools in Active Shooter and Other Armed Assailant Drills: Guidance from the National Association of School Psychologists and the National Association of School Resource Officers.* Bethesda, MD: NASP and NASRO.

Nicholls, Walter J. 2013. *The DREAMers: How the Undocumented Youth Movement Transformed the Immigrant Rights Debate.* Stanford, CA: Stanford University Press, 2013.

Oakland Public Library. N.d. "The Butterfly Effect: Art Project." Accessed November 16, 2019. http://oaklandlibrary.org/events/dimond-branch/ butterfly-effect-art-project-0.

Ofori-Atta, Akoto (project director) et al. "Since Parkland." N.d. Accessed July 1, 2019. Sinceparkland.org. In partnership with the *Miami Herald* and McClatchy.

Partnership for 21st Century Skills. 2009. *P21 Framework Definitions.* https:// files.eric.ed.gov/fulltext/ED519462.pdf.

Pratt, Charles, Sonia Gustafson, and Kurt Batdorf. 2019. "Issues That Matter: Forums Build Civic Engagement." *Public Libraries*, July/August 2019, 35–43.

Ray, Michael. 2019. "Sandy Hook Elementary School Shooting." *Britannica.* Last updated December 7, 2019. www.britannica.com/event/Newtown -shootings-of-2012.

Riggs, Krista. 2019. "Building Infrastructure to Strengthen Communities." *Public Libraries*, July/August 2019, 21–24.

Russo, Amy. 2019. "First-Grader Celebrates 7th Birthday with White House Protest." *Huffington Post*, November 11, 2019.

Sahagun, Louis. 2018. "East L.A., 1968: 'Walkout!' The Day High School Students Helped Ignite the Chicano Power Movement." *Los Angeles Times*, March 1, 2018.

Saul, Stephanie, and Anemona Hartocollis. 2018. "Too Young to Protest? 10-Year-Olds Beg to Differ." *New York Times*, March 14, 2018, A9.

Seely, Mike. 2019. "Rising Tide of Students Puts Climate Change in the Classroom." *New York Times*, June 19, 2019, A10.

Sengupta, Somini. 2019. "This Is Our Terrifying World." *New York Times*, September 21, 2019, A16.

Serrano, Alejandro. 2019. "As Thousands of Children Are Held at U.S. Border, Two East Bay Girls Are Taking Artistic Action." *San Francisco Chronicle*, November 13, 2019.

Shalby, Colleen. 2019. "Climate Activism Forged in Fire." *Los Angeles Times*, September 29, 2019, B1, B14.

Simone, Kristen. *Public Libraries as Partners in Youth Development*. 1999. New York: DeWitt Wallace–Reader's Digest Fund.

Stanford History Education Group. N.d. Civic Online Reasoning Classroom Poster. https://sheg.stanford.edu/civic-online-reasoning/classroom-poster.

Stracqualursi, Veronica. "Trump Mocks Teenage Climate Activist Greta Thunberg." CNN.com. September 25, 2019.

Su, Alice, and Ryan Ho Kilpatrick. 2019. "Hong Kong Police Target Teenagers." *Los Angeles Times*, September 28, 2019, A3.

Torres, Maria de los Angeles, Irene Rizzini, and Norma del Rio. 2013. *Citizens in the Present: Youth Civic Engagement in the Americas*. Urbana: University of Illinois Press.

Tuccillo, Diane P. 2010. *Teen-Centered Library Service: Putting Youth Participation into Practice*. Santa Barbara, CA: ABC-Clio.

Walrath, Rowan. 2018. "Supreme Court Says Kids Can Sue Trump over Climate Change." *Mother Jones*, July 31, 2018.

Walter, Virginia A. 1990. "Children as Citizens in Training: Political Socialization for a Strong Democracy." *Nonprofit and Voluntary Sector Quarterly* 19, no. 1 (Spring 1990): 7–20.

———. 2009. "Sowing the Seeds of Praxis: Incorporating Youth Development Principles in a Library Teen Employment Program." *Library Trends* 58, no. 1 (Summer 2009): 63–81.

———. 2010. *Twenty-First-Century Kids, Twenty-First-Century Librarians.* Chicago: American Library Association.

Walter, Virginia A., and Elaine Meyers. 2003. *Teens and Libraries: Getting It Right.* Chicago: American Library Association.

Warzel, Charlie. 2019. "Climate Kids and Right-Wing Media." *New York Times,* September 27, 2019, A28.

Watanabe, Teresa, Sonali Kohli, and Nina Agrawal. 2019. "Rallying to Defend 'Dreamers.'" *Los Angeles Times,* November 13, 2019, B1, B4.

Wiegand, Wayne A. 2015. *Part of Our Lives: A People's History of the American Public Library.* New York: Oxford University Press.

Williamson, Elizabeth. 2019. "When Active Shooter Drills Scare the Children They Hope to Protect," *New York Times,* September 4, 2019.

Woodhouse, Barbara. 2004. "Re-visioning Rights for Children." In *Rethinking Childhood,* edited by Peter B. Pufall and Richard P. Unsworth, 229–43. New Brunswick, NJ: Rutgers University Press.

Yenika-Agbaw, Vivian, Ruth McKoy Lowery, and Paul H. Ricks. 2018. *Using Nonfiction for Civic Engagement in Classrooms: Critical Approaches.* Lanham, MD: Rowman & Littlefield.

Yohalem, Nicole, and Karen Pittman. 2003. *Public Libraries Reflect, Retool and Reinvent Their Commitment to Young People: Lessons from the Public Libraries as Partners in Youth Development Initiative.* Washington, DC: Forum for Youth Investment.

Yoon-Hendricks, Alexandra. 2018. "Teenagers Fight Climate Change, from the Front." *New York Times,* July 28, 2018, A21.

Young, Terrell A., Barbara A. Ward, and Deanna Day. 2018. "You, Too, Can Make a Difference: Young Civil Rights Activists." In *Using Nonfiction for Civic Engagement in Classrooms: Critical Approaches,* edited by Vivian Yenika-Agbaw, Ruth McKoy Lowery, and Paul H. Ricks, 13–23. Lanham, MD: Rowman & Littlefield.

Index

A

A Is for Activist (Nagara), 31, 48
Aardema, Verna, 32, 52
activism
    books on activism and teens, 50–51
    booktalks about, 24–29
    resources on activism/children, 48–50
    resources on activism/teens, 50–51
    resources on inspiration/role models,
        51–56
    resources on war/peace, 57–61
    storytelling programs for, 30–31
    See also young activists; youth activism
Activism: The Ultimate Teen Guide (Gay),
    50
Adams, Abigail, 92–93
Adelante! Developing a Healthy Reading
    Habit initiative, 15
adolescents
    See teenagers
adult resources, 45–48
African Americans
    activism by teens, 5–6
    books on civil rights movement, 62–69
African folktales, 45
Agrawal, Nina, 7
Alexander, Kwame, 56
Ali, Muhammad
    antiwar activism by, 29
    booktalk about, 26

The Champ: The Story of Muhammad Ali
    (Bolden), 57
Twelve Rounds to Glory: The Story of
    Muhammad Ali (Smith), 61
Alice Paul and the Fight for Women's Rights
    (Kops), 92
Alva, Alfredo, 78
American Library Association (ALA)
    "Libraries Transforming
        Communities," 46
    training for community conversations,
        23
An Ample Field (Munson), 16–17
Anansi the Spider: A Tale from the Ashanti
    (McDermott), 32, 51
Anaya, Rudolfo, 81
And Tango Makes Three (Richardson &
    Parnell), 82–83
Andrew, Jared, 86
Anthony, Susan B., 93
Antiwar Activism booktalk, 29
Arno, Enrico, 45
Around America to Win the Vote: Two
    Suffragists, a Kitten, and 10,000 Miles
    (Rockliff), 92
arrests, 1
Aru Shah and the End of Time (Chokshi),
    28, 52
Ashanti tales, 45, 51
Ashman, Linda, 31, 72

Astor, Maggie, 3
Atkins, Laura
  Biddy Mason Speaks Up, 52
  Fred Korematsu Speaks Up, 58

B
Babey, Susan H., 95
Badr, Nizar Ali, 80
Batdorf, Kurt, 15
Bates, Daisy, 88
Benton Foundation, 14
Besig, Ernest, 58
Biddy Mason Speaks Up (White & Atkins), 52
Black Panthers, 6
Blitzer, Jonathan, 7
blowouts, 6
Bodart, Joni, 24
Bolden, Tonya, 26, 57
Bonnin, Jenny, 31, 75
books
  for booktalks, 30, 31
  folktales, ways to use, 32
  See also civic literacy resources
booktalks
  sample, 25–29
  as sources of civic information, 24
  storytelling programs, 30–31
Boots on the Ground: America's War in Vietnam (Partridge), 29, 57
Borreguita and the Coyote: A Tale from Ayutla, Mexico (Aardema), 32, 52
Boyce, Jo Ann, 89
Boyers, Sara Jane, 51
Braverman, Miriam, 16, 17
Bridges, Ruby
  Ruby Bridges Goes to School: My True Story, 89
  The Story of Ruby Bridges (Coles), 90
  Through My Eyes, 91
Brimmer, Larry Dane, 67
Broward County Public Library, 15
Brown, Lyn Mikel, 47
Brown, Monica, 82
Brown Berets, 6
Bruh Rabbit and the Tar Baby Girl (Hamilton), 32, 52

Bulla, Clyde, 26–27, 74
bulletin board display, 23
bullying, civic literacy resources on, 62
The Busy Tree (Ward), 30
"The Butterfly Effect: Migration Is Beautiful" initiative, 44

C
California
  DACA rights in, 7
  Dry (Shusterman), 25, 69
  fires in, global climate strikes and, 2
  young activists in, 5–6
California Endowment, 95
California State Library, 15
Can You Guess My Name? (Sierra), 32
Caps for Sale (Slobodkina), 30
Carnegie library movement, 16
Center for Civic Education
  on civic information needs of young people, 19, 20
  National Standards for Civics and Government, 9
Center for Media Literacy (CML), 10–11
Cervantes, J. C., 28, 55
The Champ: The Story of Muhammad Ali (Bolden), 26, 57
Chasing Freedom: The Life Journeys of Harriet Tubman and Susan B. Anthony, Inspired by Historical Facts (Grimes), 53
Chavez, Cesar, 81, 82
children
  civic engagement of, 35, 42–44
  civic information needs of, 19–22
  ladder of participation, 35–36
  library services for, 16–17
  political socialization of, 11–12
  resources on activism and, 48–50
  schools for, books on, 86–91
  See also young activists
Chinnam, Sriya, 3
Chokshi, Roshani, 28, 52
Christian, King of Denmark, 61
Citizens in the Present: Youth Civic Engagement in the Americas (Torres, Rizzini, & Del Rio), 12

citizenship
  civic literacy education, 8–10
  classes, 15
  DREAM Act and, 7
  voting rights for women, 93
  world citizenship, 17
civic efficacy, 10
civic engagement
  of children, 42–44
  civic literacy, components of, 35
  ladder of youth participation, 35–36
  leadership development, 40–42
  political efficacy and, 12
  public libraries as laboratories for,
    12–18
  teen advisory boards, 36–38
  volunteer opportunities, 38–40
  of young people, viii, 95–96
Civic Experience Project, 17
civic information
  booktalks as sources of, 24
  for children/teens, 19–22
Civic Lab at Skokie Public Library,
    Illinois, 16
civic literacy
  components of, 35
  definition of, 8
  education of students in, 8–10
  media literacy education, 10–11
  political socialization, 11–12
  public libraries as laboratories for,
    12–18
civic literacy resources
  activism, inspiration/role models, 51–56
  activism, war/peace, 57–61
  activism and children, 48–50
  activism and teens, 50–51
  adult resources, 45–48
  bullying, 62
  civil rights movement, 62–69
  environment, 69–76
  gun control, 76–77
  immigration issues/refugees, 77–81
  labor issues, 81–82
  LGBTQIA+ rights, 82–85
  nonviolent protest, 85–86
  schools, 86–91

  voting rights for women, 92–93
civil rights movement
  books on, 62–69
  booktalk about, 27
  middle school students and, 9
  *The Power of One: Daisy Bates and the
    Little Rock Nine* (Fradin & Fradin),
    88
Clark-Robinson, Monica, 64
Claudette Colvin: Twice toward Justice
    (Hoose), 63
Clay, Andreana, 5–6, 7–8
Cleveland Public Library
  Teen Empowerment: A Motivational
    Summit (T.E.A.M.S.), 40
  teen services of, 17
clickbait, 21–22
climate change
  books on environment, 69–76
  global climate strikes, 1–2
  Juliana v. United States, 2
Climate Change booktalk, 25–26, 31
Clinton, Hillary, 28
CML (Center for Media Literacy), 10–11
Cole, Henry, 82–83
Cole, Joanna, 31, 71
Coles, Robert, 11, 90
Columbine High School, Columbine,
    Colorado, 4
Colvin, Claudette, 63
Common Sense Fund, 3
community
  public forums at library, 23–24
  social value of public library, 13
  support of young people, 95–96
  teen volunteers and, 38–40
Community by Design project, 38
Community Conversations Workbook (ALA
    & Harwood Institute), 23–24
Conejito: A Folktale from Panama
    (MacDonald), 32, 53
Corin, Jacklyn, 77
Cornell, Joseph, 70–71
Courlander, Harold, 32, 45
Cullen, Dave, 76–77
Cunningham, Anne, 78
Curtis, Christopher Paul, 27, 67–68

Cypress Park Branch Library, Los Angeles Public Library, 38

D

DACA (Deferred Action for Child Arrivals), 7
Dain, Phyllis, 13
Danticat, Edwige, 79
Davies, Nicola, 26, 70
Davis, Angela, 5, 6
Day, Deanna, 9
de la Peña, Matt, 31, 48
Dear America: The Story of an Undocumented Citizen (Vargas), 77–78
Deedy, Carmen Agra, 61
Deferred Action for Child Arrivals (DACA), 7
Degen, Bruce, 31, 71
DeGeneres, Ellen, 28
Del Rio, Norma, 12
Delano, Marfe Ferguson, 26, 70
Demi, 85
Dennis, Jack, 11, 12
DePaola, Tomie, 55
Deporting Immigrants (Cunningham), 78
DeWitt Wallace–Reader's Digest Fund, 17
Dias, Marley
  #1000blackgirlbooks campaign, 28
  Marley Dias Gets It Done and So Can You! 50–51
digitization, 14
dignity-based rights, 42–43
DiPucchio, Kelly, 62
displays, 23
Dowell, Frances O'Roark, 29, 60
Dragon Pearl (Lee), 28, 53
Drama (Telgemeier), 83
DREAM Act (Development, Relief, and Education for Alien Minors Act), 7
A Dream of Freedom: The Civil Rights Movement from 1954 to 1968 (McWhorter), 27, 63
Dreamers, 7
Dry (Shusterman & Shusterman), 25–26, 69
DuVernay, Ava, 28

E

Earth Feeling the Heat (Guiberson), 31, 69
Earth in the Hot Seat: Bulletins from a Warming World (Delano), 26, 70
East Los Angeles Library, 43–44
Easton, David, 11, 12
education
  civic literacy education, 8–10
  media literacy education, 10–11
  schools, books on, 86–91
Edwards, Margaret, 16, 17
Eggers, Dave, 31, 49
Ehlert, Lois, 30, 73
Elegy on the Death of Cesar Chavez (Anaya), 81
Elizabeth Started All the Trouble (Rappaport), 92–93
empowered child model, 42–43
empowerment principle, 43
Engle, Margarita, 96
Enoch Pratt Library, Baltimore
  Civic Experience Project, 17
  teen services of, 16
Enriquez, Gaspar, 81
environment
  civic literacy resources on, 69–76
  Climate Change booktalk, 25–26, 31
  open information environment, 22–24
  Trees and Environmental Activism booktalk, 26–27, 30
Epstein, Su, 47
equality principle, 42
Evans, Shane
  Lillian's Right to Vote: A Celebration of the Voting Rights Act of 1965 (Winter), 65
  We March, 31, 68
events, for leadership development, 40–41

F

fake news
  library warning about, 20–21
  as problematic, 22
Falkowski, Melissa, 77
Farris, Christine King, 65
Faulkner, Matt, 92–93
Fisher, Leonard Everett, 85

5A's of Media Literacy, 21
folktales
  The Hat-Shaking Dance and Other
    Ashanti Tales from the Gold Coast
    (Courlander), 45
  Peace Tales: World Folktales to Talk About
    (MacDonald), 46
  storytimes with, 30
  ways to use, 32–33
Fourteenth Amendment, 93
Fradin, Dennis Brindell, 88
Fradin, Judith Bloom, 88
The Fragile Flag (Langton), 57
Francisco, Grace, 15
Fred Korematsu Speaks Up (Atkins & Yogi),
  58
Free as a Bird: The Story of Malala (Maslo),
  86
Free Library of Philadelphia, 40–41
"free speech" bulletin board, 23
Freedman, Russell
  Freedom Walkers: The Story of the
    Montgomery Bus Boycott, 64
  Vietnam: A History of the War, 29, 61
  We Will Not Be Silent: The White Rose
    Student Resistance Movement that
    Defied Adolf Hitler, 61
Freedom Walkers: The Story of the
  Montgomery Bus Boycott (Freedman),
  64
Freedom's Children: Young Civil Rights
  Activists Tell Their Own Stories
  (Levine), 64
Frier, Raphaële, 88
Fronty, Aurelia, 88
fundraising, 37

G
Gaia Warriors: Urgent: The Fight Is On!
  (Davies), 26, 70
Galt, Margot Fortunato, 29, 60
Gandhi (Demi), 85
Gandhi (Fisher), 85
Gandhi, Mahatma, 85–86
Gandhi: The Young Protester Who Founded
  a Nation (Wilkinson), 85–86
Garcetti, Eric, 5

Garfield High School, East Los Angeles,
  California, 6
Gay, Kathlyn, 50
Gay & Lesbian History for Kids: The
  Century-Long Struggle for LGBT
  Rights (Pohlen), 83
gay rights, 82–85
gay students, 7–8
George (Gino), 83–84
Gerber, Carole, 30, 71
Gibbons, Gail, 26–27, 74
Gilliland, Judith Heide, 59–60
Gino, Alex, 83–84
global climate strikes, 1–2
global warming
  books on, 69–70, 73–76
  Climate Change booktalk, 25–26, 31
González, Emma
  activism by, 3
  Parkland (Cullen), 76–77
Goodall, Jane, 75
government
  civic literacy and, 8–10
  political socialization and, 11–12
Graegin, Stephanie, 62
grants
  for leadership development, 41
  for TAB projects, 38
Great Depression
  public libraries in, 13
  young adult services in, 17
Greenstein, Fred I., 11
Grimes, Nikki, 53
Gross, Melissa, 20
Groundbreaking Guys: 40 Men Who
  Became Great by Doing Good
  (Peters), 26, 54
Gubnitskaia, Vera, 47
Guerrero, Diane, 79
Guevara, Che, 5
Guiberson, Brenda Z., 31, 69
gun control
  active shooter drills, 4–5
  civic literacy resources on, 76–77
  Parkland students, activism by, 3–4
Gun Control (Otfinoski), 76
Gustafson, Sonia, 15

H

Hale, Christy, 91

Hamilton, Virginia, 32, 52

Harrod, Kerol, 46

Hart, Roger, 35–36

Hartocollis, Anemona, 3

Harvesting Hope: The Story of Cesar Chavez (Krull), 81

Harwood Institute for Public Innovation
"Libraries Transforming Communities," 46
training for community conversations, 23

The Hat-Shaking Dance and Other Ashanti Tales from the Gold Coast (Courlander), 32, 45

Heart on Fire: Susan B. Anthony Votes for President (Malaspina), 93

Hector: A Boy, a Protest, and the Photograph that Changed Apartheid (Wright), 87

Heide, Florence Parry, 59–60

The Help Yourself Cookbook for Kids: 60+ Easy Plant-Based Recipes Kids Can Make to Stay Healthy and Save the World (Roth), 70

Herthel, Jessica, 84

hip-hop generation, 6

Hispanic Unity of Florida, 15

Hoe, Denise, 1

Hogg, David, 3, 76–77

homophobia, 7–8

Hong Kong, 1

Hood, Susan, 55

Hoose, Philip, 63

Hopkins, H. Joseph, 74–75

Horn, Zoia, 22

How the Ladies Stopped the Wind (McMillan), 27, 70

Hudson, Cheryl Willis, 56

Hudson, Wade, 56

Huneck, Stephen, 31, 73

Hunter-Gault, Charlayne, 66–67

Hussey, Kristin, 4

I

I Am Jazz (Herthel & Jennings), 84

I Am Malala: How One Girl Stood Up for Education and Changed the World (Yousafzai with McCormick), 87

I Walk with Vanessa: A Story about a Simple Act of Kindness (Kerascoët), 62

immigration
Butterfly Effect initiative, 44
civic literacy resources on, 77–81
José de la Luz Sáenz and, 60
young activists and, 6–7

imposed queries, 20

individualism principle, 42

information for young activists
booktalks, sample, 25–29
booktalks as sources of civic information, 24
civic information for children/teens, 19–22
folktales, ways to use, 32–33
open information environment, 22–24
storytelling programs, 30–31

information requests, 22

Ingraham, Laura, 2

inspiration, resources on, 51–56

internet
online information, evaluation of, 20–21
public libraries and, 14

Iqbal
Malala, a Brave Girl from Pakistan/Iqbal, a Brave Boy from Pakistan: Two Stories of Bravery, 81–82
story of, 28–29

"Issues That Matter" forums, 15

J

Jack Outwits the Giants (Johnson), 32, 54

Jarvie, Jenny, 3

Jennings, Jazz, 84

John Muir: My Life with Nature (Cornell), 70–71

Johnson, Jen Cullerton, 27, 73

Johnson, Paul Brett, 32, 54

Johnston, Tony, 32, 55

Jones, Mother, 82

José de la Luz Sáenz, 60

Julian Is a Mermaid (Love), 31, 84

Juliana v. United States, 2

Just a Minute: A Trickster Tale and Counting Book (Morales), 32, 54

K
Kai, Hanane, 80
Kaia and Lillian (child activists), 44
Keats, Ezra Jack, 31, 73
Kerascoët, 62, 88
Kids Care! 75 Ways to Make a Difference for People, Animals, and the Environment (Olien), 31, 71
Kilpatrick, Ryan Ho, 1
Kimmel, Elizabeth Cody, 86
King, Martin Luther, Jr.
  books on civil rights movement, 62–66, 68–69
  Boots on the Ground: America's War in Vietnam (Partridge), 57
  opposition to Vietnam War, 29
Kiyoko (child activist), 44
Knight, Margy Burns, 80–81
Koester, Amy, 16
Kohli, Sonali, 5, 7
Kops, Deborah, 92
Korematsu, Fred, 58
Kramer, Ann, 54
Krull, Kathleen, 81
Kulling, Monica, 82

L
La Frontera: El Viaje con Papá | My Journey with Papa (Mills & Alva), 78
LA Times, 2
labor issues, 81–82
Ladd, London, 65
ladder of youth participation, 35–36
Langton, Jane, 57
Last Stop on Market Street (De la Pena), 31, 48
Latinx community
  immigration issues/refugees, books on, 77–81
  labor issues, books on, 81–82
Latinx teens
  activism by, 5, 6
  civic engagement of children, program for, 43–44

youth activism for immigration rights, 6–7
leadership development, 40–42
Leading Tens from Voluntarism to Activism booktalk, 25
Leaf Jumpers (Gerber), 30, 71
LEAP (Literacy Enrichment Afterschool Program), 40–41
Lee, Milly, 59
Lee, Yoon Ha, 28, 53
Leigh, Robert D., 12–13
Leonard, Tom, 75
Lerner, Sarah, 77
lesbian rights, 82–85
Let the Children March (Clark-Robinson), 64
Letters from Wolfie (Sherlock), 29, 58
Levine, Ellen, 64
Levinson, Cynthia, 69
Levy, Debbie, 89
Lewin, Ted, 59–60
LGBTQIA+
  public libraries and, 8
  rights, books on, 82–85
librarians
  active shooter training for, 4–5
  booktalks, sample, 25–29
  booktalks as sources of civic information, 24
  civic engagement of children and, 42–44
  civic engagement of young people and, viii, 95–96
  civic information needs of children/teens, 19–22
  open information environment, 22–24
  storytelling booktalks, 30–31
  teen services and, 17–18
  volunteers, working with, 38–40
libraries
  See public libraries
"Libraries Transforming Communities" (ALA & Harwood Institute for Public Innovation), 23–24, 46
library faith, 13, 16
library staff, 4–5

Library Youth Outreach: 26 Ways to Connect with Children, Young Adults and Their Families (Harrod & Smallwood), 46
Lillian's Right to Vote: A Celebration of the Voting Rights Act of 1965 (Winter), 65
Lin, Maya, 57
literacy
    See civic literacy; media literacy education
literature, 9
Little Tokyo Branch, Los Angeles Public Library, 38
Lopez, Steve, 5
Los Angeles, California
    DACA rights, youth activism for, 7
    youth activism against gun violence, 5
Los Angeles Public Library
    teen volunteers at, 38–40
    Teens Leading Change program, 35, 38
    West Covina branch, TABs of, 37–38
Louder Than Guns campaign, 5
Love, Jessica, 31, 84
Lowery, Lynda Blackmon, 67
Lowery, Ruth McKoy, 9, 47–48
Lowry, Lois, 59

M
Maathai, Wangari, 27, 73
MacDonald, Margaret Read
    Conejito: A Folktale from Panama, 32, 53
    Peace Tales: World Folktales to Talk About, 46
    Shake-It-Up Tales: Stories to Sing, Dance, Drum, and Act Out, 47
The Magic School Bus and the Climate Challenge (Cole & Degen), 31, 71
Magoon, Kekla, 90–91
Malala, a Brave Girl from Pakistan/Iqbal, a Brave Boy from Pakistan: Two Stories of Bravery (Winter), 29
Malala: A Hero for All (Sayles), 87–88
Malala: Activist for Girls' Education (Frier), 88
Malala's Magic Pencil (Yousafzai), 88
Malaspina, Ann, 93
Malcolm X, 5

Mama Miti: Wangari Maathi and the Trees of Kenya (Napoli), 72, 73
Mama's Nightingale: A Story of Immigration and Separation (Danticat), 79
Mandela, Nelson, 54–55
Mandela: The Hero Who Led His Nation to Freedom (Kramer), 54
March for Our Lives, 3
March On! The Day My Brother Martin Changed the World (Farris), 65
Marching with Aunt Susan: Susan B. Anthony and the Fight for Women's Suffrage (Murphy), 93
Marjory Stoneman Douglas High School, Parkland, Florida
    books about gun control, 76–77
    young activist survivors of shooting, vii
    young activists after shooting, 3–4
Marley Dias Gets It Done and So Can You! (Dias with McGowan), 28, 50–51
Martinez, Pete, 6
Maslo, Lina, 86
Mayer, Robert H., 27, 68
Mbalia, Kwame, 56
McCabe, Ronald, 13–14
McCormick, Patricia, 87
McCully, Emily Arnold, 74
McDermott, Gerald, 32, 51
McDonald, Country Joe, 29, 57
McDonnell, Patrick, 72
McGowan, Siobhán, 50–51
McKay, Kim, 31, 75
McMillan, Bruce, 27, 70
McWhorter, Diane, 27, 63
Me . . . Jane (McDonnell), 72
Media Literacy and the Emerging Citizen: Youth, Engagement and Participation in Digital Culture (Mihailidis), 46
media literacy education
    civic information needs of young people, 19–22
    library support of, 20
    principles of, 10–11
Merolli, Kiyoki, 8
Meyers, Elaine, 41–42
migrant children, 44

Mihailidis, Paul
  5A's of Media Literacy, 21
  Media Literacy and the Emerging Citizen: Youth, Engagement and Participation in Digital Culture, 46
  on media literacy education principles, 10–11
Milk, Harvey, 84–85
Miller, C., 10
Mills, Deborah, 78
Moeller-Peiffer, Kathleen, 4
Molz, Redmond Kathleen, 13
monarch butterflies, 44
Moore, Anne Carroll, 16
Morales, Yuyi
  Harvesting Hope: The Story of Cesar Chavez, 81
  Just a Minute: A Trickster Tale and Counting Book, 32, 54
Morgan, Lori A.
  on civic literacy, 10
  on Project Citizen findings, 9
Moroz, Erica, 79
Morrison, Frank, 64
Muhammad Ali and Other Male Activists booktalk, 26
Muir, John, 70–71
Multicultural Alliance, 5–6
Munson, Amelia, 16–17
Murphy, Claire Rudolf, 93
My Family Divided (Guerrero with Moroz), 79

N
Nagara, Innosanto, 31, 48
Namugerwa, Leah, 1–2
Napoli, Donna Jo, 72, 73
National Association for Media Literacy Education (NAMLE)
  on media literacy education principles, 10–11
  poster about online information evaluation, 20–21
National Association of School Psychologists, 4
National Association of School Resource Officers, 4

National School Walkout (March 2018), 3
National Standards for Civics and Government (Center for Civic Education), 9, 19
National Youth Administration, 13
needs-based rights, 42–43
Nelson Mandela: Long Walk to Freedom (Mandela), 55
Never Too Young: 50 Unstoppable Kids Who Made a Difference (Weintraub), 48–49
New York Public Library, 16, 17
New York Times, 1–2
Newtown, Connecticut, 4
Nicholls, Walter J., 7
Nim and the War Effort (Lee), 59
Nineteenth Amendment, 43, 92
Ninth Circuit Court of Appeals, 2
No One Is Too Small to Make a Difference (Thunberg), 26, 72
nonfiction
  for civic literacy education, 9
  Using Nonfiction for Civic Engagement in Classrooms: Critical Approaches (Yenika-Agbaw, Lowery, & Ricks), 47–48
nonviolent protest
  books on civil rights movement, 62–69
  books on war/peace activism, 57–61
  civic literacy resources on, 85–86
Number the Stars (Lowry), 59
nursery rhyme/song/movement activity, 30

O
Oakland, California
  homophobia issue for teens in, 7–8
  students of color in, 5–6
Oakland Public Library, 44
obligations, 35
O'Brien, Anne Sibley, 80–81
Oceanside Public Library, 15
Ofori-Atta, Okoto, 5
Okeke, Tyler, 5
Olcott, Frances Jenkins, 16
Olien, Rebecca, 31, 71

On Our Way to Oyster Bay: Mother Jones and Her March for Children's Rights (Kulling), 82
One Crazy Summer (Williams-Garcia), 65–66
#1000blackgirlbooks campaign, 28
Online Activism: Social Change through Social Media (Vink), 25, 51
online information, evaluation of, 20–21
open information environment, 22–24
Otfinoski, Steven, 76
Other Words for Home (Warga), 79–80

P
Pacoima Branch Library, Los Angeles Public Library, 38
Palisades Charter High School, Los Angeles, California, 5
Pallotta, Jerry, 27, 75
Pankhurst, Emmeline, 92
Parkland (Cullen), 76–77
Parkland High School shooting
   books about gun control, 76–77
   young activist survivors of, vii
   young activists after, 3–4
Parkland Speaks: Survivors from Marjory Stoneman Douglas Share Their Stories (Lerner), 77
Parnell, Peter, 82–83
participation
   See youth participation
participation, ladder of, 35–36
Partnership for 21st Century Skills, 8, 9
partnerships, 15, 17
Partridge, Elizabeth, 29, 57
The Past Is Our FUTURE project, 38
Paths to Peace: People Who Changed the World (Zalben), 26, 59
Paul, Alice, 92
Paul, Caroline, 25, 49–50
peace, resources on, 57–61
Peace Tales: World Folktales to Talk About (MacDonald), 46
Peaceful Fights for Equal Rights (Sanders), 86
Peters, Stephanie True, 26, 54
Pew Charitable Trust, 9
Pinkney, Andrea Davis, 66

Pittman, Karen, 96
A Place to Land: Martin Luther King Jr. and the Speech That Inspired a Nation (Wittenstein), 66
A Planning Process for Public Libraries (Public Library Association), 14
PLPYD (Public Libraries as Partners in Youth Development), 17–18, 96
Plummer, Mary Wright, 16
Pohlen, Jerome, 83
Political Activism: How You Can Make a Difference (Schwartz), 49
political efficacy, 12
political socialization, 11–12
pop-ups, 16
Portland, Oregon, 3
poster, 20–21
The Power of One: Daisy Bates and the Little Rock Nine (Fradin & Fradin), 88
Powered by Girl: A Field Guide for Supporting Youth Activists (Brown), 47
Pratt, Charles, 15
Pride: The Story of Harvey Milk and the Rainbow Flag (Sanders), 84–85
print resources, viii–ix
   See also civic literacy resources
privacy principle, 43
programming, 37
Project Citizen, 9–10
The Promise of Change: One Girl's Story in the Fight for School Equality (Boyce & Levy), 89
protection principle, 43
protest, nonviolent
   books on civil rights movement, 62–69
   books on war/peace activism, 57–61
   civic literacy resources on, 85–86
public forums, 23–24
public libraries
   active shooter training for library staff, 4–5
   booktalks, sample, 25–29
   booktalks as sources of civic information, 24
   civic engagement of children and, 42–44
   civic engagement of young people and, 95–96

civic information needs of young
people, 19–22
as laboratories for civic literacy/
engagement, 12–18
leadership development, 40–42
open information environment,
creation of, 22–24
teen advisory boards, 36–38
volunteers, teen, 38–40
young activists and, vii–viii
Public Libraries, 15
Public Libraries as Partners in Youth
Development (PLPYD), 17–18, 96
Public Library Association, 14

R
race/ethnicity, 5–6
Rain! (Ashman), 31, 72
Rappaport, Doreen, 92–93
Ray, Michael, 4
reading, public library programs for, 17
recommendations
See civic literacy resources
Red Leaf, Yellow Leaf (Ehlert), 30, 73
refugees, 77–81
Refugees and Migrants (Roberts), 80
resources
civic information needs of young
people, 19–22
resource list, viii–ix
See also civic literacy resources
Reynolds, Peter H., 49
Richardson, Justin, 82–83
Ricks, Paul H., 9, 47–48
Riggs, Krista, 15
rights
books on civil rights movement, 62–69
of children, 42–43
information about, 35
LGBTQIA+ rights, resources on, 82–85
voting rights for women, 92–93
Riordan, Rick, 28
Rizzini, Irene, 12
Roberts, Ceri, 80
Rochelle, Belinda, 27, 68–69
Rockliff, Mara, 92
Rockwell, Anne E., 31, 76
role models, 51–56

Roth, Ruby, 70
Ruby Bridges Goes to School: My True Story
(Bridges), 89
Ruiz, Sil, 43–44
"Run, Hide, Fight" model, 4
Russo, Amy, 8
Ruurs, Margriet, 80

S
Sahagun, Louis, 6
Sala, Felicita, 82
Salazar, Adriana, 2
Sally Goes to the Beach (Huneck), 31, 73
Sami and the Time of the Troubles (Heide &
Gilliland), 59–60
San Diego County Health and Human
Services Agency's Public Health
Department, 15
Sanders, Bob, 86
Sanders, Rob, 84–85
Sandy Hook Elementary School,
Newtown, Connecticut, 4
Santa Cruz (CA) Public Library, 37
Saul, Stephanie, 3
Say Something (Reynolds), 49
Sayles, Elizabeth, 87–88
school shootings
active shooter drills, 4–5
gun control, books on, 76–77
Parkland High School shooting,
survivors of, vii
at Sandy Hook Elementary School, 4
young activists and, 3–4
schools
books on, 86–91
safety of, 3–5
Schwartz, Heather E., 49
SCLC (Southern Christian Leadership
Conference), 68
The Sea of Monsters (Riordan), 28
Seeds of Change (Johnson), 27, 73
Seely, Mike, 3
Sendak, Maurice, 56
Sengupta, Somini, 2
*Separate Is Never Equal: Sylvia Mendez and
Her Family's Fight for Desegregation*
(Tonatiuh), 90
Serrano, Alejandro, 44

Sessions, Katherine Olivia, 74–75
Shake-It-Up Tales: Stories to Sing, Dance, Drum, and Act Out (MacDonald), 47
Shaking Things Up: 14 Young Women Who Changed the World (Hood), 55
Shalby, Colleen, 2
Sherlock, Patti, 29, 58
Shooting the Moon (Dowell), 29, 60
Shusterman, Jarrod, 69
Shusterman, Neal, 25–26, 69
Shuttlesworth, Fred, 68
Side by Side: The Story of Dolores Huerta and Cesar Chavez | Lado a Lado: La Historia de Dolores Huerta y Cesar Chavez (Brown), 82
Sierra, Judy, 32
Silvey, Anita, 75
Simone, Kristen, 17
"Since Parkland" project, 5
Sit-In: How Four Friends Stood Up by Sitting Down (Pinkney), 66
Skokie Public Library, Illinois, 16
Slobodkina, Esphyr, 30
Smallwood, Carol, 46, 47
Smith, Charles R., 26, 29, 61
Sno-Isle Libraries, Washington, 15
Snopes.com, 21
The Snowy Day (Keats), 31, 73
Social Justice and Activism in Libraries: Essays on Diversity and Change (Epstein, Smallwood, & Gubnitskaia), 47
social media
  civic literacy and, 10
  media literacy and, 21–22
  Online Activism: Social Change through Social Media (Vink), 51
social value, of public library, 13
Soldier for Equality: José de la Luz Sáenz and the Great War (Tonatiuh), 60
songs, 30, 31
Southern Christian Leadership Conference (SCLC), 68
Squirrel and John Muir (McCully), 74
standards, 9
Stanford History Education Group, 20–21
Staub, Leslie, 79

Stepping Stones: A Refugee Family's Journey (Ruurs), 80
Stewart, Kate, 8
Stop This War! American Protest of the Conflict in Vietnam (Galt), 60
Stories for "Woke" Children and Their Parents booktalk, 31
The Storm Runner (Cervantes), 28, 55
The Story of Ruby Bridges (Coles), 90
storytelling programs
  Climate Change booktalk, 31
  folktales, ways to use, 32–33
  related to activism, 30–31
  Trees and Environmental Activism booktalk, 30–31
Stracqualursi, Veronica, 2
students
  activism by students of color, 5–6
  civic information needs of, 19–22
  civic literacy education, 8–10
  media literacy education, 10–11
  political socialization of, 11–12
  public library's role in civic literacy/ engagement, 12–18
Su, Alice, 1
suffrage movement
  books on voting rights for women, 92–93
  Chasing Freedom: The Life Journeys of Harriet Tubman and Susan B. Anthony, Inspired by Historical Facts (Grimes), 53
Super Manny Stands Up! (DiPucchio), 62
Superheroes in Fantasy and Real Life booktalk, 28–29
The Surrender Tree (Engle), 96

T
The Tale of Rabbit and Coyote (Johnson), 32, 55
A Taste of Freedom: Gandhi and the Great Salt March (Kimmel), 86
technology, 14
teen advisory boards (TABs)
  examples of, 37–38
  organization of, 36–37
Teen Empowerment: A Motivational Summit (T.E.A.M.S.), 40

Teen Justice, 5–6
teen leadership assistants (TLAs), 41
teen leadership summit, 41
Teen Power Politics: Make Yourself Heard (Boyers), 51
teenagers
    civic engagement of, 35, 95–96
    civic information needs of, 19–22
    ladder of participation, 35–36
    leadership development by, 40–42
    library services for, history of, 16–18
    political socialization of, 11–12
    resources on activism and teens, 50–51
    teen advisory boards, 36–38
    volunteer opportunities for, 38–40
    See also young activists; youth activism
Teen-Centered Library Services: Putting Youth Participation into Practice (Tuccillo), 36, 47
Teens and Libraries: Getting It Right (Walter & Meyers), 41–42
Teens Leading Change program, 35, 38
Telgemeier, Raina, 83
Tell Me, Tree: All about Trees for Kids (Gibbons), 26–27, 74
Through My Eyes (Bridges), 91
Thunberg, Greta
    global climate strike and, 1–2
    No One Is Too Small to Make a Difference, 26, 72
    Parkland survivors and, vii
TLAs (teen leadership assistants), 41
To the Mountaintop: My Journey through the Civil Rights Movement (Hunter-Gault), 66–67
Today the World Is Watching You: The Little Rock Nine and the Fight for School Integration 1957 (Magoon), 90–91
Todos Iguales: Un Corrido de Lemon Grove / All Equal: A Ballad of Lemon Grove (Hale), 91
Tonatiuh, Duncan
    Separate Is Never Equal: Sylvia Mendez and Her Family's Fight for Desegregation, 90
    Soldier for Equality: José de la Luz Sáenz and the Great War, 60
Torres, Maria de los Angeles, 12

Trace, 5
A Tree Is a Plant (Bulla), 26–27, 74
A Tree Is Nice (Udry), 30
The Tree Lady: The True Story of How One Tree-Loving Woman Changed a City Forever (Hopkins), 74–75
Trees and Environmental Activism booktalk
    for grade 2 or 3, 26–27
    for preschool storytime, 30–31
trickster tales
    The Hat-Shaking Dance and Other Ashanti Tales from the Gold Coast (Courlander), 45
    Just a Minute: A Trickster Tale and Counting Book (Morales), 54
    use of, 32
Tristan Strong Punches a Hole in the Sky (Mbalia), 56
True Green Kids: 100 Things Kids Can Do to Save the Planet (McKay & Bonnin), 31, 75
Trump, Donald, 2
Tuccillo, Diane, 36, 47
Tudor, Aslan, 76
Turning 15 on the Road to Freedom: My Story of the 1965 Selma Voting Rights March (Lowery), 67
Twelve Days in May: Freedom Ride 1961 (Brimmer), 67
Twelve Rounds to Glory: The Story of Muhammad Ali (Smith), 26, 29, 61
Twenty-First-Century Kids, Twenty-First-Century Librarians (Walter), 42, 96
Tyler, Dillon, 3

U

Udry, Janice May, 30
The Undefeated (Alexander), 56
undocumented immigrants
    books on, 77–79
    youth activism for immigration rights, 7
United Nations Committee on the Rights of the Child, 2
United States, Juliana v., 2
Untamed: The Wild Life of Jane Goodall (Silvey), 75

US Department of Education, 9
Using Nonfiction for Civic Engagement in Classrooms: Critical Approaches (Yenika-Agbaw, Lowery, & Ricks), 9, 47–48

V
Vargas, Jose Antonio, 77–78
Vietnam: A History of the War (Freedman), 29, 61
Vietnam War
  Antiwar Activism booktalk, 29
  Boots on the Ground: America's War in Vietnam (Partridge), 57
  The Champ: The Story of Muhammad Ali (Bolden), 57
  Letters from Wolfie (Sherlock), 58
  Muhammad Ali and Other Male Activists booktalk, 26
  Shooting the Moon (Dowell), 60
  Stop This War! American Protest of the Conflict in Vietnam (Galt), 60
  Vietnam: A History of the War (Freedman), 61
Villasenor, Alexandria, 2
Vink, Amanda, 25, 51
Vista Library, San Diego, CA, 39, 40
volunteers
  Leading Tens from Voluntarism to Activism booktalk, 25
  TAB participation, 36–38
  volunteer opportunities, 38–40
voting process, 43
voting rights
  Lillian's Right to Vote: A Celebration of the Voting Rights Act of 1965 (Winter), 65
  Turning 15 on the Road to Freedom: My Story of the 1965 Selma Voting Rights March (Lowery), 67
  When the Children Marched: The Birmingham Civil Rights Movement (Mayer), 68
  for women, resources on, 92–93

W
walkouts, 6
Wallace, Chad, 69

Walrath, Rowan, 2
Walter, Virginia A.
  introduction, vii–ix
  on leadership development by TLAs, 41
  on political efficacy, 12
  Teens and Libraries: Getting It Right, 41–42
  Twenty-First-Century Kids, Twenty-First-Century Librarians, 42
war, books on, 57–61
Ward, Barbara A., 9
Ward, Jennifer, 30
Warga, Jasmine, 79–80
Warzel, Charlie, 2
Watanabe, Teresa, 7
The Watsons Go to Birmingham—1963 (Curtis), 27, 67–68
We Are All in the Dumps with Jack and Guy: Two Nursery Rhymes with Pictures (Sendak), 56
We March (Evans), 31, 68
We Rise, We Resist, We Raise Our Voices (Hudson & Hudson), 56
We Say #NeverAgain: Reporting by the Parkland Student Journalists (Falkowski), 77
We Will Not Be Silent: The White Rose Student Resistance Movement that Defied Adolf Hitler (Freedman), 61
Weintraub, Aileen, 48–49
West Covina branch, Los Angeles County Library System, 37–39
Westwood Teens, 38
What Can a Citizen Do? (Eggers), 31, 49
When the Children Marched: The Birmingham Civil Rights Movement (Mayer), 27, 68
White, Arisa, 52
Who Belongs Here? An American Story (Knight), 80–81
Who Will Plant a Tree? (Pallotta), 27, 75
Why Are the Ice Caps Melting? The Dangers of Global Warming (Rockwell), 31, 76
Wiegand, Wayne A., 13, 17
Wilkinson, Philip, 85–86
Williams, Mabel, 16
Williams-Garcia, Rita, 65–66
Williamson, Elizabeth, 4

Winter, Jeannette, 29, 81–82
Winter, Jonah, 65
Witness to Freedom: Young People Who Fought for Civil Rights (Rochelle), 27, 68–69
Wittenstein, Barry, 66
"woke children," stories for, 31
Wolstein, Joelle, 95
women, voting rights for, 92–93
Wood, Michele, 53
Woodhouse, Barbara, 42–43
Works Progress Administration (WPA), 13
workshop, 41
World War I, 13
Wright, Adrienne, 87

Y
The Yellow Star: The Legend of King Christian X of Denmark (Deedy), 61
Yenika-Agbaw, Vivian, 9, 47–48
Yogi, Stan, 58
Yohalem, Nicole, 95–96
Yoon-Hendricks, Alexandra, 3
You Are Mighty: A Guide to Changing the World (Paul), 25, 49–50
Young, Terrell A., 9
young activists
    active shooter drills and, 4–5
    gay teens, 7–8
    global climate strike, 1–2
    gun violence and, 4–5
    in Hong Kong, 1
    immigration rights as focus, 6–7
    Juliana v. United States, 2
    overview of chapters on, viii–ix
    Parkland High School shooting and, 3–4
    students of color, 5–6
    Virginia A. Walter on, vii
    younger children as activists, 8
young activists, information for
    booktalks, sample, 25–29
    booktalks as sources of civic information, 24
    civic information for children/teens, 19–22
    folktales, ways to use, 32–33
    open information environment, 22–24
    storytelling programs related to activism, 30–31
Young Adult Library Services (journal), 18
Young Water Protectors: A Story about Standing Rock (Tudor), 76
The Youngest Marcher: The Story of Audrey Faye Hendricks, a Young Civil Rights Activist (Levinson), 69
Yousafzai, Malala
    Free as a Bird: The Story of Malala (Maslo), 86
    I Am Malala: How One Girl Stood Up for Education and Changed the World, 87
    Malala, a Brave Girl from Pakistan/Iqbal, a Brave Boy from Pakistan: Two Stories of Bravery (Winter), 81
    Malala: A Hero for All (Sayles), 87–88
    Malala: Activist for Girls' Education (Frier), 88
    Malala's Magic Pencil, 88
    story of, 28, 29
youth activism
    books on activism and children, 48–50
    booktalks about, 24–29
    civic literacy, understanding/implementing, 8–12
    overview of chapter on, viii
    public libraries as laboratories for civic literacy/engagement, 12–18
    young activists today, 1–8
youth advisory boards, 18
Youth Council to End Gun Violence, 5
youth organizations, 12
youth participation
    civic engagement of children, 42–44
    ladder of participation, 35–36
    leadership development and, 40–42
    teen advisory boards, 36–38
Youth Participation Worksheet, 41–42

Z
Zalben, Jane Breskin, 26, 59
Zero Hour, 3